Crafts

JOY
to the World
a Treasury of Christmas Crafts

CREATIVE
PUBLISHING
international

Copyright © 1998 Creative Publishing international, Inc.
5900 Green Oak Drive, Minnetonka, Minnesota 55343 • 1-800-328-3895 • All rights reserved • Printed in U.S.A

TABLE OF *Contents*

GIFTS *for* GIVING

Santa's not the only one busy making gifts this year! Your family and friends will be thrilled when they see the delightful presents you've made for them. Make a Grandma's L'il Angel Bib for the youngest member of the family, or a Christmas Tic-Tac-Toe Board for an older child. The Celestial Candleholder will be a welcome gift in any home, and someone would just love to wear the festive Appliquéd Holly Pantsuit.

CELESTIAL
Candleholder

Blue and gold are the colors of the heavens, which we turn toward with our prayers and dreams. This candleholder can be the answer to your prayers for a quick, yet stylish, gift that you have only dreamed of. Paint and rag a wooden base to look like burled maple, wrap a pillar candle in wire mesh, and add a ribbon and star trims to complete.

MATERIALS

- Wooden octagon candle plate 7" x 8" x .75" (18 x 20.5 x 2 cm)*
- 4 wooden snowflake/star ornaments, 4" x 5½" (10 x 14 cm), ¼" (6 mm) thick*
- Artist's brush: fine liner, 1" (2.5 cm) sponge
- Acrylic craft paints: buttercrunch, rose, metallic gold
- Maple wood stain
- 12" (30.5 cm) of 20-gauge gold wire
- 1" (2.5 cm) wide masking tape
- 8" x 9½" (20.5 x 24.3 cm) aluminum dia-mond wire mesh*
- 10" (25.5 cm) wooden dowel, ¼" (6 mm) diameter
- 18" (46 cm) gold ribbon, 2" (5 cm) wide
- 6" (15 cm) pillar candle, 3" (7.5 cm) diameter
- Pattern Sheet
- Miscellaneous items: fine sandpaper, tack cloth, paint palette, tracing and transfer paper, pencil, plastic wrap, old credit card, wire cutters, needlenose pliers

*(See Sources on page 159 for purchasing information.)

1 Preparation: Refer to page 156 for Painting Instructions and Techniques. Lightly sand wooden candle plate and stars; remove dust with tack cloth. Basecoat candle plate top only (not the candle insert hole) and the stars on the front, back and edges with buttercrunch paint using a 1" (2.5 cm) sponge brush. Basecoat the candle insert hole and the candle plate sides with rose paint. Let dry; sand lightly and repeat, except paint over the rose on the sides of the candle plate with butter-crunch and paint star edges with metallic gold.

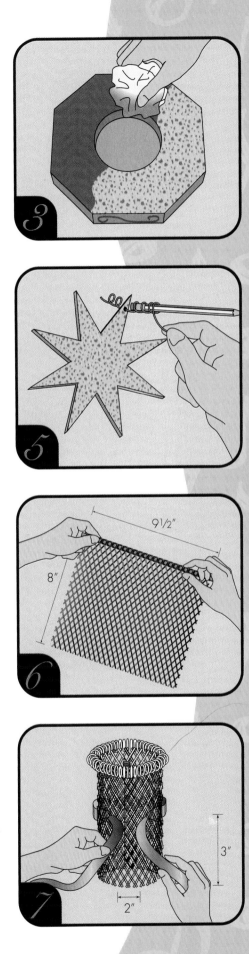

2 Candle Plate: Trace the curlicue pattern to tracing paper. Transfer the pattern to the four 4" (10 cm) long sides of the candle plate, or paint 3" (7.5 cm) curlicues freehand with the liner brush and metallic gold paint.

3 Faux Finish: Apply maple stain with sponge brush or a soft cloth to the candle plate top. Crumple up a 6" (15 cm) strip of plastic wrap in your hand. Refer to the Step 3 illustration to dab up and down on the stained area. The plastic wrap removes some of the stain, letting the paint show through, to give the appearance of burled maple. Refer to the photo and continue ragging off the stain until satisfied with the finish. Let dry overnight.

4 Gold Border: Refer to the photo to tape around the candle plate, making a 1" (2.5 cm) border. Use a credit card to rub along the outer edge of the masking tape; make sure it adheres well so the paint won't seep under. Use the sponge brush to paint the border with metallic gold. Remove tape carefully.

5 Stars: Repeat Step 3 to faux finish the star fronts. Cut four 2" (5 cm) pieces of 20-gauge gold wire for hangers. Insert 1 wire piece into a star and wrap the wire coming out the back 2 times around the liner brush handle. Refer to the Step 5 illustration to wrap the front of the wire in the same way, and make a small hook at the end for hanging on the wire mesh.

6 Wire Mesh: Cut a piece of wire mesh 8" (20.5 cm) tall and 9½" (24.3 cm) wide with wire cutters or old scissors. See the Step 6 illustration to make sure the diamond pattern is going vertically along the 8" (20.5 cm) edge. Place the mesh on a flat work surface, and place the wooden dowel along a 9½" (24.3 cm) edge. Roll the mesh 1 time completely around the dowel as shown in the illustration; remove the dowel. Use two 2" (5 cm) pieces of 20-gauge gold wire to join the wire mesh together in 2 spots— see the Step 7 illustration—wrapping 3 times in 1 diamond. Trim wire ends and use needlenose pliers to tuck under.

7 Finishing: Refer to the photo to weave the ribbon in and out of the diamonds in the mesh, making 4 loops on the outside. See the Step 7 illustration to begin and end about 1" (2.5 cm) to the right of the center front and 3" (7.5 cm) from the bottom of the mesh; tie a bow. Insert a candle by gently sliding the wire mesh, with the roll at the top, over the candle until the bottom edge of the mesh is flush with the candle bottom. Place the wire-mesh-covered candle in the base; hang on the 4 stars. Never leave lit candle unattended.

PIN-WOVEN
Christmas Cards

Pin weaving is a technique in which pins are used to hold the warp ribbons in place, while you weave the weft ribbons over and under to create one-of-a-kind greetings to special friends.

MATERIALS

For Each Card
- 5" x 7" (12.5 x 18 cm) blank greeting card with envelope
- 8" (20.5 cm) square ½" (1.3 cm) grid paper*
- 6" (15 cm) square fusible interfacing
- 10" (25.5 cm) square heavy cardboard or foamboard
- Glues: fabric, hot glue gun

For Tree Card
- 3 yd. (2.75 m) each ½" (1.3 cm) single-fold bias tape: red, green
- ½ yd. (0.5 m) red gimp braid, ¼" (6 mm) wide
- 2" (5 cm) square gold fabric

For Star Card
- 1½ yd. (1.4 m) gold single-fold bias tape, ½" (1.3 cm) wide
- 1½ yd. (1.4 m) gold grosgrain ribbon, ⅝" (1.5 cm) wide
- 1 yd. (0.95 m) gold gimp braid, ¼" (6 mm) wide

For Bell Card
- ⅝" (1.5 cm) grosgrain ribbon: 1½ yd. (1.4 m) each green, gold; 2 yd. (1.85 m) red
- ½ yd. (0.5 m) green gimp braid, ¼" (6 mm) wide
- Artificial berries and greens
- Dried natural baby's breath
- Pattern Sheet
- Miscellaneous items: tracing paper, pencil, scissors, ruler, straight pins, iron

* (See Sources on page 159 for purchasing information.)

TREE CARD

1 Trace the 5 patterns to tracing paper, placing tree and bell patterns on the fold, and cut out. See the Step 1 illustration to center grid paper on cardboard. Center fusible interfacing, fusible side up, on grid paper; pin. Cut 6" (15 cm) lengths of green bias tape. Align bias tape on vertical grid lines, abutting edges. Pin at top and bottom of grid, angling pins away from center.

2 Begin at bottom to weave lengths of red bias tape over and under green to opposite edge; trim. Weave next strip under and over to opposite edge. Continue weaving, alternating over and under, and keeping strips level and close together. Use wool setting with steam to fuse the woven bias tape while pinned to the board. Remove pins, turn and press from other side.

3 Pin the tree pattern to pin-woven ribbons, aligning grainline with the green ribbon vertical weave; cut out as shown in the Step 3 illustration. Use fabric glue to apply red gimp braid around cut edges. Cut the small star pattern from gold fabric. Center and glue tree and star to front of card.

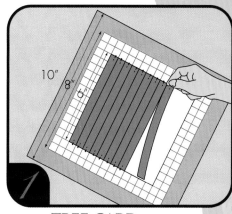

TREE CARD

BELL CARD

1 Follow Step 1 of Tree Card. Cut red, green and gold ribbons into 6" (15 cm) lengths. Alternate and align on vertical grid lines, abutting edges. Follow Step 2 of Tree Card to weave alternating red, green and gold ribbons through vertical ribbons and to fuse them.

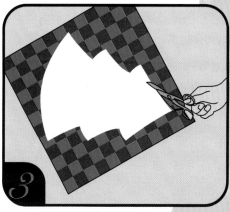

TREE CARD

2 Cut the bell and clapper patterns from pin-woven ribbons, aligning grainlines with vertical weave. Use fabric glue to apply green gimp braid around cut edges of bell and curved edge of clapper. Glue clapper under bottom edge of bell. Center and glue bell to card front. Tie remaining red ribbon into a 2-loop bow and glue to center top of bell. Hot-glue greenery, berries and baby's breath to center of bow.

STAR CARD

1 Refer to Steps 1 and 2 of the Tree Card to weave gold grosgrain ribbon through 6" (15 cm) lengths of gold bias tape on vertical grid and to fuse them.

STAR CARD

2 Cut 1 large and 2 small stars from pin-woven ribbons, aligning grainlines with vertical weave. Use fabric glue to apply gold gimp braid around cut edges of large star as shown in the Step 2 illustration. Refer to the photo to glue stars to front of card.

Precious ANGEL PIN

With a handful of stars from heaven, this angel can't wait to grace a holiday wardrobe. Made from opaque shrink plastic, with gold-trimmed wings and locks of golden wire, she will garner many compliments. Give away angel pins as gifts, but be sure to keep one for yourself.

MATERIALS

For One 2½" (6.5 cm) Angel Pin
- Opaque shrink plastic, 1 sheet
- Markers: ultra fine-point permanent black, extra fine-point metallic gold, fine-point violet blue
- Soft-lead colored pencils: pink, peach, raspberry
- ⅛" (3 mm) paper punch
- 2⅓ yd. (2.17 m) 28-gauge gold wire
- 1½" (3.8 cm) pin back
- Heavy-duty adhesive
- Pattern Sheet
- Miscellaneous items: scissors, wire cutters, large needle, nonstick baking sheet, oven

1 Preparation: Follow manufacturer's instructions on how to use shrink plastic. Place shrink plastic sheet over 5 pattern pieces and trace design onto shrink plastic with black marker. See the Step 1 illustration.

2 Coloring: Use colored pencils to shade the face and hands peach, the lips raspberry and the cheeks pink. Color eyes with violet blue marker. Use fine-line metallic gold marker to outline just inside black traced wing line. Color stars gold.

3 Baking: Carefully cut out all pieces with scissors. Refer to the pattern and Step 3 illustration to punch holes in head for hair using paper punch. Place all 5 pattern pieces on a baking sheet, colored side up. Follow manufacturer's instructions for baking time and temperatures. Remove from oven; let cool.

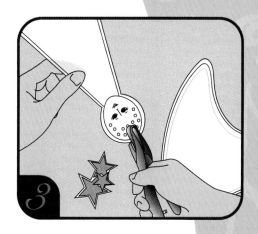

4 Hair: Use wire cutters to cut 24 lengths of gold wire each 3½" (9 cm) long. Wrap half of each length around needle in a tight corkscrew to curl; see Step 4 illustration. For center curls, insert straight end through hole to back, then through next hole to front; curl end around needle. For edge curls, insert straight end through hole and curl end around needle; bend curl to front. Place 2 curls in each hole.

5 Assembly: Refer to the photo to apply adhesive and glue wings to body back and arms to body front. Glue stars to hands. Glue pin back vertically to back of wings.

All-American SCOOTER

Once they find it, you'll never get your kids off this scooter.
It's Santa's country version of the metal scooters we
remember from the good old
days, but this is easy to make
with simple woodworking skills.
Tie on the beaded handlebar
tassels, and let 'em ride!

1 Mitering: Use the miter box and saw and follow the Step 1 illustration to cut 45° angles in the bumper and both braces. Also cut 1 end of the base to match the angled bumper; see the photo and Step 2 illustration.

MATERIALS

- Pine wood: 24" (61 cm) of a 2" x 6" (5 x 15 cm) for the base; 84" (213.5 cm) of a 2" x 2" (5 x 5 cm) cut into: 14" (35.5 cm) for the handlebar; 5½" (14 cm) for the bumper; two 8" (20.5 cm) lengths for the braces; two 24" (61 cm) lengths for the front bars
- 26" (66 cm) wood dowel, 1" (2.5 cm) in diameter
- Tools: miter box and saw; drill with ⁵/₃₂", ⁷/₃₂", 1" and countersink bits; screwdriver
- Wood screws: 6 No. 10 flat-head, 3" (7.5 cm); 4 No. 10 flat-head, 2¼" (6 cm); 2 No. 10 flat-head, 2½" (6.5 cm); 8 No. 12 round-head, 1" (2.5 cm)
- 2½" (6.5 cm) rigid coaster wheels, two
- Maple wood stain
- Patriotic stencil with a 1½" (3.8 cm) wide design
- Stencil paint: red, white, blue
- Paintbrushes: stencil, ¾" (2 cm) flat
- Waterbase varnish
- 5 yd. (4.6 m) white leather lacing
- 28 each pony beads: red, white, blue
- Miscellaneous items: tape measure, fine sandpaper, tack cloth, soft cloth, scissors

2 Drilling: See the Step 2 illustration to drill holes in the base top and the handlebar bottom in the following order: At red dots, drill through wood with 5/32" bit. At blue dots, drill through wood with 7/32" bit. On base, countersink holes on bottom; on handlebar, countersink holes on top. At yellow circles, drill 1" (2.5 cm) deep using 1" drill bit, drilling over previous holes. Use the 7/32" bit to drill 1½" (3.8 cm) centered holes into ends of the dowel and both front bars.

3 Staining: Sand all wood surfaces; wipe with tack cloth. Use soft cloth to apply stain to all surfaces, following manufacturer's instructions. Let dry overnight.

4 Assembly: Place the bumper on top rear of base, matching angled edges. Follow the Step 2 illustration to mark the 2 screw holes on the bumper and drill through the wood with a 5/32" bit. Attach bumper to base with the two 2½" (6.5 cm) flat screws, screwing from the bumper down into the base. Insert dowel in 1" (2.5 cm) holes in base and handlebar. Use the 3" (7.5 cm) screws to attach the front bars and the center dowel to the base and the handlebar.

5 Braces: Position each brace between front bar and the base. Mark 1¼" (3.2 cm) up from brace ends along the upper edge. Use the 7/32" bit to drill 2 pilot holes on each brace, drilling slightly into the front bars and base. Countersink and attach with 2¼" (6 cm) screws.

6 Stenciling: Refer to the photo to stencil a patriotic design on front and back of handlebar, top of braces, top and back of bumper, front bars and base sides. Let dry overnight. Apply 2 coats of varnish with the flat brush; let dry between coats.

7 Bead Tassels: Cut leather lacing into six 30" (76 cm) lengths. Inserting from the bottom, thread 1 length into each handlebar hole. Slide on a bead and insert end down through the same hole; use 1 bead of each color on each handlebar end. At each end, string 3 groups of red, white and blue beads on 1 lacing, spacing at irregular intervals; knot after each group. Repeat to string 2 bead groups on each remaining lacing. Double-knot lacing ends.

8 Wheels: See the Step 8 illustration to mount the wheels on the bottom of the base. Center wheels and drill 8 pilot holes with 7/32" bit. Attach each wheel with four 1" (2.5 cm) screws.

READY-TO-WEAR
Gingerbread

If you'd rather craft your gingerbread men than bake them, follow this easy recipe. Without even turning on the oven, these gingerbread men are easy to decorate—using dimensional paints for white icing and red cinnamon hearts. Finally, sprinkle with "Noel" wishes and your shirt is ready to wear!

MATERIALS

- Red cotton shirt with button placket
- Dimensional fabric paints: white, Christmas green, black, Christmas red, pink, golden brown iridescent
- Golden brown iridescent brush-on fabric paint
- 1/8 yd. (0.15 m) 45" (115 cm) red/white stripe cotton fabric
- 1/8 yd. (0.15 m) ultra-hold fusible web
- Expandable sponge
- Miscellaneous items: pencil, scissors, pinking shears, ruler, tracing paper, stylus (or dry ballpoint pen), white chalk, T-shirt board, disposable palette, water container, paper towels, iron, hair dryer

1 Striped Fabric Rectangles: Fuse web to the wrong side of red/white stripe fabric. Use the pinking shears to cut four 3" x 4" (7.5 x 10 cm) fabric rectangles with lengthwise stripes. Follow manufacturer's instructions and refer to the photo to fuse 2 fabric rectangles lengthwise on each side of button placket.

2 Patterns: Trace the gingerbread boy and the lettering patterns onto tracing paper. Trace the gingerbread boy onto sponge, and cut out.

3 Sponging Gingerbread: Insert T-shirt board into shirt. Place sponge in water to expand; dry with paper towels. Squeeze brown brush-on paint onto palette. Using a thick coat of paint, sponge a gingerbread centered on each fabric rectangle. You may choose to practice sponging on some scrap fabric first. Use the hair dryer to speed drying time.

4 Painting Noel: Trace "noel" lettering on wrong side of tracing paper with chalk. Position pattern chalk side down, with "noel" centered below a fabric rectangle. Use the stylus or dry pen to trace over lines, transferring pattern. Repeat below each rectangle. Use dimensional white to paint lettering and the dots; see the Step 4 illustration.

5 Painting Gingerbread: Refer to the photo and gingerbread pattern to use dimensional paints; let dry between each color. Follow manufacturer's recommendations and drying times. Use white to paint wavy icing lines on the gingerbread and outline rectangles; be sure to cover pinked fabric edges. Paint pink cheeks on gingerbread and wavy lines around button placket. Paint red noses, smiles, and mini hearts on chests. Paint a green leaf on each side of hearts. Dot black eyes close together. Outline each gingerbread with brown.

6 Holly: See the Step 6 illustration and the photo to paint holly with pink berries and green leaves. Use the Holly A pattern randomly above the gingerbread design. Use a complete Holly B design between each "noel", and a partial Holly B on each end. Paint random white dots above gingerbread and white highlights on berries below.

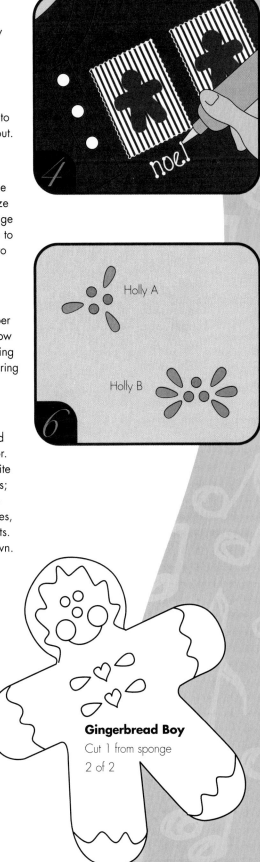

Holly A

Holly B

Gingerbread Boy
Cut 1 from sponge
2 of 2

READY-TO-WEAR GINGERBREAD PATTERNS

Lettering Pattern
Trace 1 to tracing paper
1 of 2

noel

SAUCER
Votives

These clever candleholders are just what Santa ordered for the holidays, because they can be made so quickly from inexpensive materials. Take them along as hostess gifts, make them for the kids' teachers who deserve so much more, or set them on your dining room table as favors at your next gathering.

MATERIALS

For Both Votives
- Votive candle
- Reindeer moss
- Dried florals:
  For A: 3 sprigs pepperberries, 4 sprigs lavender, 3 sprigs red yarrow
  For B: 3 sprigs each blue hydrangea and lavender
  For C: 1 rosebud, 4 fresh seeded eucalyptus leaves, 2 sprigs pepperberries, 2 sprigs blue hydrangea, 3 sprigs lavender, 2 fresh seeded eucalyptus pods
  For D: 2-3 sprigs pepperberries, 2 sprigs fresh seeded eucalyptus pods

For E: 3 sprigs pepperberries, 4 sprigs white hydrangea
- Hot glue gun
- Natural raffia, 12" (30.5 cm) for glass votive, 8" (20.5 cm) for terra-cotta votive

For Glass Votive
- 4" terra-cotta saucer
- Glass votive candleholder

For Terra-Cotta Votive
- 2" (5 cm) terra-cotta pot
- 3" (7.5 cm) terra-cotta saucer
- Miscellaneous items: kitchen sink, glass cleaner, scissors, ruler

GLASS VOTIVE

1 Preparation: Wash the terra-cotta saucer with warm water; let dry thoroughly. Use glass cleaner or vinegar and water to thoroughly clean the glass votive candleholder. Hot-glue the glass votive candleholder onto the terra-cotta saucer, placing the votive candleholder off center, as shown in the Step 1 illustration.

2 Moss: Break off small clumps of the reindeer moss. Hot-glue the moss to the terra-cotta saucer all around the votive candleholder. Do not cover the saucer completely.

3 Finding Florals: Purchase dried florals at your local craft store, or use fresh flowers from your yard or garden that you have dried. Fresh pepperberries and fresh seeded eucalyptus are available from your local florist. If you choose to use dried pepperberries, you may want to enhance their color with a little raspberry red paint.

4 Assembly: Refer to the photo and the Step 4 illustration to hot-glue florals to the moss. For B, hot-glue 3 sprigs each of lavender and hydrangea evenly around the candleholder. For C, hot-glue 1 rosebud in the center and 2 eucalyptus leaves on each side. Randomly hot-glue around blue hydrangea, pepperberries, lavender and eucalyptus pods. For D, hot-glue 3 sprigs of pepperberries evenly around the candleholder, and 2 sprigs of eucalyptus pods between.

5 Finishing: Cut 12" (30.5 cm) of raffia, 3-4 strands thick. Tie raffia into a small bow and glue to the base of the votive candleholder. Place candle in the candleholder. Always snuff out candle before wick has burned completely. Never leave a burning candle unattended.

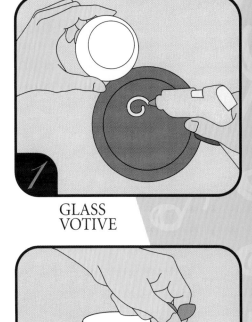

GLASS VOTIVE

GLASS VOTIVE

TERRA-COTTA VOTIVE

1 Assembly: Repeat Step 1 of Glass Votive to wash both terra-cotta pot and saucer and hot-glue terra-cotta pot to the **center** of the terra-cotta saucer.

2 Assembly: Repeat Steps 3 and 4 of Glass Votive. For A, hot-glue 3 sprigs of pepperberries and 3 sprigs of red yarrow evenly around; add 4 sprigs of lavender randomly. For E, hot-glue 3 sprigs of pepperberries evenly around, and 4 sprigs of white hydrangea randomly around.

3 Finishing: Cut 8" (20.5 cm) of raffia, 2 strands thick. Refer to the photo and the Step 3 illustration to tie raffia into a knot around the top of the pot. Place candle in the candleholder.

TERRA-COTTA VOTIVE

Grandma's L'il ANGEL BIBS

Loving stitches are all you need to make one of Grandma's L'il Angel Bibs. Look for a cotton terry bib with a Christmas design, or stitch it on a solid white. Your little angel will make it through meals with clean clothes and you'll be in the holiday spirit all season long.

MATERIALS

For Each Bib
- Christmas print or white cotton terry bib with 14-count Aida insert
- 1 skein each of 6-strand DMC embroidery floss in colors listed on Color Key
- No. 24 tapestry needle
- Scissors

ANGEL BIB STITCH CHARTS

Color Key
- ■ 321 Christmas Red
- ■ 353 Peach Flesh
- ■ 434 Light Brown
- ■ 700 Bright Christmas Green
- ■ 726 Lt. Topaz
- ■ 832 Golden Olive
- ■ 948 Lt. Peach Flesh
- — 3799 Dk. Pewter Gray Backstitches

Refer to the Cross-Stitch General Instructions and Stitches on page 155 and the Stitch Charts above to cross-stitch the design using 2 strands of floss. Work all backstitches using 1 strand of Vy. Dk. Pewter Gray No. 3799.

PAPER SANTA
Trimmings

Mix cotton paper in your blender to mold a Victorian Santa; you'll be amazed how many ways you can add an old-world touch on a papier mâché box, a special gift, holiday bag, greeting card or place card for your Christmas dinner. Metallic paints, glitter, beads and ribbons are just a few ideas to accent this Santa.

MATERIALS

For Each Project
- 1 sheet Cotton Press® linter paper and additive*
- Victorian Santa terra-cotta clay mold*
- Glues: white craft glue, hot glue gun
- 6" (15 cm) white or gold paper doily for the Box and Card
- Paints: gold and green glitter, gold spray, assorted watercolors for the Painted Santa

For Box
- 8" (20.5 cm) papier mâché box
- Trims: gold ribbons: 1 yd. (0.95 m), 1" (2.5 cm) wide; ¼ yd. (0.25 m), ¼" (6 mm) wide; small ribbon roses

For Package
- Gift wrap to cover box
- Trims: ½ yd. (0.5 m) Christmas ribbon, 1½" (3.8 cm) wide; ½ yd. (0.5 m) gold cord; 3 gold jingle bells

For Gift Bag
- Solid-color gift bag
- Christmas print fabric or gift wrap to fit front of bag

For Each Card
- 6" x 12" (15 x 30.5 cm) card stock
- 6 mm gold beads, approximately 12

For Painted Santa
- Acrylic spray sealer
- Miscellaneous items: scissors, large bowl, measuring cup and spoons, strainer, electric blender, sponge, paper towels, black permanent marker, double-stick transparent tape, pinking shears (for the gift bag)

*(See Sources on page 159 for purchasing information.)

1 Preparation: Follow manufacturer's instructions or prepare paper and molds as follows. Place 1 cotton linter sheet and 1 tsp. (5 mL) additive in blender with water; blend on high for 1 minute. Prepare clay Santa mold by rinsing with water. Lightly spray with vegetable oil, then quickly rinse off most of the oil with warm water. Pour out 1/3 of the water from blender through a strainer into a bowl, leaving enough water so pulp is still very wet.

2 Molding: Pour enough pulp from strainer so mold is thinly covered, about 2/3 to 1 cup (150 to 250 mL). Spread pulp with a knife, letting it flow out on edges to create a lacy look. See the Step 2 illustration to soak up excess water with a sponge. Press pulp firmly into mold with fingertips or paper towel to set details.

3 Unmolding: Place mold near a heat vent, in the sun, in the oven at 300°F (150°C) for 35-40 minutes, or in the microwave on high for 2 minutes. Let cotton dry completely until it is crispy. Gently remove Santa from the mold by sliding a thin-bladed knife under edges. Leave lacy edges, as for gift bag and painted Santa, or trim with a scissors.

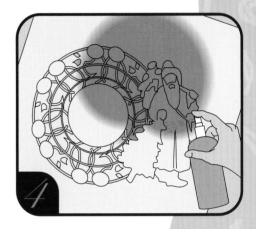

4 Papier Mâché Box: See the Step 4 illustration to spray box, lid and Santa with gold; let dry. Center doily on lid top; use craft glue to glue doily and Santa. Glue wide gold ribbon around lid lip. Tie roses into a bouquet with narrow gold ribbon; hot-glue to lid as shown.

5 Gift Package: Lightly spray Santa with gold paint. Brush gold glitter paint on tree, beard, and hat and boot trims. Tie gold cord and ribbon into a single bow; knot cord ends. Hot-glue bow to package, 3 bells in center of bow, and Santa below bow.

6 Gift Bag: Use pinking shears to trim fabric rectangle to fit bag front. Center, and use craft glue to glue fabric and Santa.

7 Cards: Fold card stock in half. Center and glue doily on front. Lightly spray paint Santa with gold, and glue to center of card. Brush tree with glitter paint and glue on pearls, as shown in the Step 7 illustration.

8 Painted Santa: Lightly spray Santa with acrylic spray to seal. Refer to the photo and paint lightly with thinned watercolors.

BUTTON VEST
& Jewelry

What's round or flat, has holes or shanks and never seems to go out of style? Buttons, of course! No wardrobe is complete without this vest, necklace and earrings. The "lapels" of a denim vest are covered with buttons for a fun and fashionable look. Coordinate it with a necklace strung with buttons to look like precious ivory. While you're in the button mode, whip up some earrings to match.

MATERIALS

For Earrings
- ¾" (2 cm) earring backs, 1 pair
- White buttons: two 1½" (3.8 cm) flat; two ¾" (2 cm) shank; eight ½" (1.3 cm) oval shank; eight ⅜" (1 cm) shirt
- Ultra-hold clear adhesive

For Necklace
- Two-hole flat buttons: ivory: ⅝" (1.5 cm), 18; ¾" (2 cm), 20; 1" (2.5 cm), 24; 1⅛" (2.8 cm), 14; white: ⅜" (1 cm), 62; ½" (1.3 cm), 114
- ⅝" (1.5 cm) round white shank button
- 4½ yd. (4.15 m) heavy cotton thread
- Large-eyed tapestry needle
- Clear nail polish

For Vest
- Purchased denim vest
- Assorted white and ivory buttons, 100 to 120
- Air-soluble marker
- Ultra-hold clear adhesive
- Miscellaneous items: sewing needle, white thread, scissors, wire cutters

EARRINGS

Refer to the photo and the Earrings illustration to make the earrings. Use wire cutters to remove the shanks from 3/4″ and 1/2″ (2 and 1.3 cm) shank buttons. Glue 3/4″ (2 cm) buttons to the center front of 1 1/2″ (3.8 cm) buttons. Evenly space and glue 4 oval buttons around the 3/4″ (2 cm) button. Glue 4 shirt buttons between oval buttons. Glue earring back to back of 1 1/2″ (3.8 cm) button.

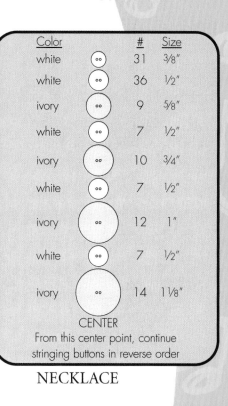

EARRINGS

NECKLACE

1 Stringing: Cut thread in half. Double-thread needle with 1 length and knot ends. Leave a 5″ (12.5 cm) tail and string buttons on thread in order and numbers as shown in the Necklace illustration. Leave tail and cut needle from thread. Double-thread needle with second length of thread and knot ends. String buttons through second holes.

2 Closure: At 1 end of necklace, tie threads in an overhand knot to make a 3/4″ (2 cm) loop. Push buttons close to knotted loop. Knot threads at opposite end and attach shank button with a square knot. Trim threads close to knots. Paint knots with clear nail polish to secure. Insert shank button through loop to close.

Color		#	Size
white	∘∘	31	3/8″
white	∘∘	36	1/2″
ivory	∘∘	9	5/8″
white	∘∘	7	1/2″
ivory	∘∘	10	3/4″
white	∘∘	7	1/2″
ivory	∘∘	12	1″
white	∘∘	7	1/2″
ivory	∘∘	14	1 1/8″

CENTER
From this center point, continue
stringing buttons in reverse order

NECKLACE

VEST

Use air-soluble marker to draw lapel outlines on vest front. Lay out buttons in a pleasing arrangement on lapel to fill it in. It is okay if there are gaps—another layer on top will cover those. Sew bottom button layer by hand using ivory or white thread. Glue additional button layers on top of the sewn layer to cover the gaps and provide an interesting design and texture.

VEST

Christmas House
NIGHT-LIGHT

This plastic house decorated with glass paints will delight everyone on your gift list. Placed over a night-light, it is all set for the holidays, from the candles in the window to the wreath on the door. It looks just like one of those Christmas village collectibles, but will mean so much more, because you have done it yourself.

MATERIALS

- 1 Gallery Glass™ plastic house*
- 1 bottle Gallery Glass™ liquid leading*
- 1 bottle each Gallery Glass Window Colors™ in colors listed on Color Key*
- Hot glue gun
- Pattern Sheet
- Miscellaneous items: tracing paper, red pencil, masking tape, paint palette, toothpicks, large box, 6 cardboard pieces at least 6" x 9" (15 x 23 cm), cotton swabs, craft knife
- *(See Sources on page 159 for purchasing information.)

1 Pattern: Trace 4 pattern pieces with red pencil to tracing paper. Tape House Side pattern piece to cardboard—it will let you turn the project without moving the house pieces—and place on a flat and level work surface. Clean plastic house pieces with soap and mild water to remove dust; do not use window cleaner or any abrasive.

2 Leading: See the Step 2 illustration to trace over the solid lines on the pattern with the liquid leading, following manufacturer's instructions. Make sure that all lead lines are joined to prevent paint colors from seeping into adjoining areas. To correct mistakes, lift off wet leading with a cotton swab, or cut out dry leading with a craft knife, being careful not to scratch plastic. Let dry at least 8 hours before painting.

3 Painting: Follow the Pattern Sheet and paint; the numbers on the Color Key are the last 2 digits of the paint color. Apply paint directly from the bottle around the leading lines. Fill in the center with a generous amount of paint, almost as high as the leading lines. Clean up paint that gets onto leading with cotton swabs.

4 Combing: Stroke back and forth quickly in straight lines with a toothpick. This gives the paint a smooth grain. Comb all colors except crystal clear. After applying paint to a few areas, pick up the cardboard and tap firmly underneath painted areas to remove air bubbles.

5 Roof and House Sides: Place rectangle Roof pieces, **beveled edges down,** over the patterns. Lead the top edges, shingles from top to the bottom, and bottom edge; paint top to bottom. Place square House Side pieces, **grooved side and beveled edge down,** over the patterns. Lead in order: top edge, left bricks, candles, windows, bushes, bottom edge, right bricks. Paint in the same order, doing the walls last.

6 House Back and Front: Place pieces, **beveled edges down,** over the patterns. The House Back is the piece with the hole; see the Step 2 illustration. Lead the Back in order: top edge, timbers, light hole, left bricks, candle, window, tree, right bricks and bottom edge. Lead the Front in order: top edge; timbers; left bricks, window and bush; wreath; door; right window, bush and bricks; and bottom edge. Paint each in leading order, doing the walls last.

7 Wall Assembly: Assemble house in the cardboard box; see the Step 7 illustration to place a House Side piece painted side against box. Place House Front, painted side against the box, near it on another side. Hot-glue along the groove and slide the Front piece into the groove. Move the house to the next box corner, and repeat to glue the House Back. Apply hot glue to both grooves on the other House Side, and complete.

8 Roof Assembly: Hold a roof in each hand and place on the house, joining at the top. Remove 1 piece, holding the other in place. Apply hot glue along the joining line, and put the other Roof piece on, gluing them together. Lift off the roof, as shown in the Step 8 illustration, and apply hot glue to the top peaked edges of the House Front and Back. Place roof back on, being careful to center it.

JINGLE ELVES
Necklace

MATERIALS

- 10 mm round wood beads: 3 natural, 2 green, 1 red; 8 mm round wood beads: 66 natural, 8 green, 4 red
- 3/8" (1 cm) wood barrel beads, 3 natural
- 3/8" (1 cm) gold jingle bells, six
- 4 mm gold beads, 50
- 3 mm pom-poms: 2 red, 1 green
- Small felt pieces: red, green
- White craft glue
- 3 yd. (2.75 m) monofilament
- White chenille stem
- Fine-line permanent-ink markers: green, red, black
- Clear water-base varnish or sealer
- Small paintbrush
- Miscellaneous items: scissors, tracing paper, pencil, wire cutters, ruler, sewing needle, sandpaper

For the youngest on your Christmas list, you can quickly string this adorable wood bead necklace. Older children will enjoy being one of Santa's elves, and they can make this necklace all by themselves to give as a gift to friends or to younger siblings.

1 Hat: Trace the hat pattern onto tracing paper and cut 2 green and 1 red from felt. Overlap and glue straight edges to form a cone. Glue a red pom-pom to each green hat and a green one to the red hat.

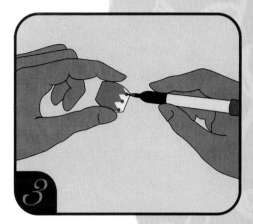

2 Head: Insert and glue chenille stem end into 10 mm natural bead hole for the beard. Bend in a curve to reach opposite hole. Cut, leaving enough to insert in hole, and glue. Make 3 heads. Glue hats to top of head beads. Use the black marker to make 2 dots for the eyes.

3 Body: See the Step 3 illustration to color 2 barrel beads green with red dots for each green elf and 1 barrel bead red with green dots for the red elf. Apply coat of varnish or sealer with small paintbrush; let dry.

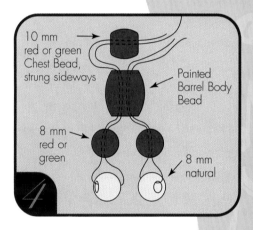

4 Stringing Elves: See the Step 4 illustration throughout. Cut two 6″ (15 cm) pieces of monofilament. Center one 8 mm natural bead for foot on each piece and knot. To make each leg, thread both monofilament ends through an 8 mm red bead for a red elf and a green bead for a green elf. Thread all 4 monofilament ends through a matching painted barrel body bead. Thread 2 ends through a sideways 10 mm matching bead for the chest. Tie together at the side with remaining 2 ends; conceal knot inside bead. Trim ends. Lightly sand top of chest bead. Glue head bead with matching hat to sanded chest bead; let dry.

5 Stringing Necklace: Cut a 5-ft. (4.6 m) length of monofilament and fold it in half, using both cut ends to string beads. String beads as shown in the Step 5 illustration. The Red Elf is the center of the necklace; reverse the beads shown in order to complete the other half of the necklace. Knot, conceal and trim monofilament ends.

HAT PATTERN

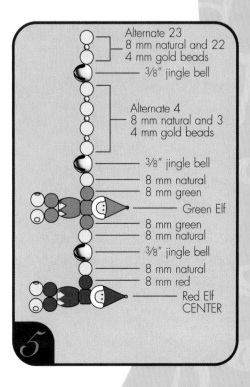

"TO MY TEACHER"
Gift Boxes

When the Christmas gift list gets really long, you'll appreciate these easy-to-make gift boxes. Tuck a little something inside the papier-mâché box you paint yourself, and the kids' teachers will put you on the honor roll for sure.

1 Preparation: See page 156 for Painting Instructions and Techniques. Use a ruler to mark a 3/16" (4.5 mm) border on box lid. Use No. 4 brush to basecoat the border and sides of lid with cadmium yellow/antique gold mix, and rest of lid with black green. Trace pattern to tracing paper and transfer to lid with white graphite paper.

2 Apple: Use the No. 4 brush to basecoat the apple country red and leaf with leaf green. Mix 3 parts gold with 1 part terra-cotta and basecoat stem.

3 Apple Highlighting: Refer to the Step 3 illustration to use shader brush and cadmium orange to highlight top edge and right side of apple, and under the line where stem and apple meet. Highlight top edge and leaf vein with bright green.

4 Apple Shading: Use shader brush and russet to shade the following: left side and bottom edge of apple; under leaf; above line where stem and apple meet; bottom leaf edge; behind leaf vein, left side of stem; circle at top of stem. Shade bottom edge of lid sides terra-cotta.

5 Pine Branches: Use liner brush to paint pine branches forest green, then leaf green. Use shader brush to shade pine branches black green. Dot country red berries in pine branches.

6 Finishing: Use liner brush and buttermilk to paint lettering and dots. See the Step 6 illustration. Highlight right side of apple, leaf and stem. If desired, use black permanent marker to sign and date box on bottom or under lid, or to write a message to the teacher. Spray all painted surfaces with acrylic varnish.

PAINTING PATTERNS

ELEGANT
Decoupage Candleholders

Make this trio of candleholders in varying heights for the mantel or a matched pair of Elegant Decoupage Candleholders for a centerpiece. The choice is yours, as you cut a potato chip can to size, decoupage on a design from a Christmas card and decorate with trims. This is truly a recycled Christmas project!

MATERIALS

For Each Candleholder
- Empty potato chip can
- Christmas card with musical theme
- Sheet music, 2¾" x 5" (7 x 12.5 cm)
- Paints: dark green acrylic, iridescent glitter fabric
- Paintbrushes: 2" (5 cm) sponge, 1" (2.5 cm) flat
- Trims: ⅔ yd. (0.63 m) gold braid, ½" (1.3 cm) wide; 1 yd. (0.95 m) each: gold lamé ribbon, ½" (1.3 cm) wide; red satin ribbon, ⅛" (3 mm) wide; ¾ yd. (0.7 m)

gold twist cord; 3" (7.5 cm) mini musical instrument; 5" (12.5 cm) mini berry pick; green excelsior
- Glues: decoupage glue, hot glue gun
- 3" (7.5 cm) drinking glass with 2½" (6.5 cm) diameter graduated bottom
- Dark green votive candle
- Miscellaneous items: ruler, pencil, serrated knife, scissors, paper towels, craft knife, emery board

1 Design: Choose Christmas card design; it should cover ⅓ to ½ of can. Make card easier to work with by inserting tip of craft knife into edge of card and peeling away the back. See the Step 1 illustration to cut out the design with the craft knife.

2 Base: Cut potato chip can at the top to desired height with serrated knife and sand edge with emery board to smooth. Wipe can clean with damp paper towel. Use sponge brush to basecoat with dark green; let dry 1 hour between coats. Repeat to apply 3 coats.

3 Decoupaging: Use sponge brush to apply 1 coat of decoupage glue to can; let dry. Brush a thin coat of glue onto the back of the design and onto the side of can in an area slightly larger than the design. Position design on can ¼" (6 mm) from bottom rim. Coat entire surface of can with glue as shown in the Step 3 illustration. Let dry; apply second coat. Hot-glue gold braid around top and bottom of can.

4 Sheet Music: Brush sheet music with decoupage glue; let dry and repeat to coat other side. Wrap bottom edge of music around pencil to curl forward and top edge to curl backward; see the Step 4 illustration. Angle music scroll on can with top corner even with can top; hot-glue. Cluster some excelsior strands with berry pick. Refer to the photo to hot-glue to top braid at side of music scroll.

5 Bow: Cut 24" (61 cm) of red satin ribbon. Loop with gold cord and lamé ribbon twice to make bow; tie together with remaining 12" (30.5 cm) of red ribbon. Knot ends of gold cord. Hot-glue bow on top of excelsior and pick. Twist and loop lamé tails around can; spot-glue and trim as needed. Hot-glue instrument to bow center, slightly overlapping edge of music scroll.

6 Finishing: Lightly brush glitter fabric paint over candleholder with flat brush, including instrument and sheet music; let dry. Insert glass with votive candle in top of can. Never leave lit candle unattended.

Christmas
TIC-TAC-TOE

Everyone will think the elves were working overtime when they see this adorable game. Three stars or three trees in a row, instead of X's and O's, wins in this Christmas version of tic-tac-toe. A simple blanket stitch around a pinked edge of fused fabric and felt finishes the game; it even has a storage pocket in the back. It is so cute, you may not even want to wrap it.

MATERIALS

- 9" x 12" (23 x 30.5 cm) felt sheets: 2 cranberry and 1 each: lime green, yellow, denim blue, sage green
- Two 9" (23 cm) squares dark red cotton print fabric
- 1¼ yd. (1.15 m) fusible web
- Flat red buttons: twelve ¾" (2 cm), four ½" (1.3 cm)
- 1 skein DMC 6-strand red embroidery floss, to match the cranberry felt
- Embroidery needle
- Miscellaneous items: tracing and transfer paper, pencil, ruler, straight pins, iron, press cloth, scissors, pinking shears, craft knife, cutting surface

1 Cutting and Preparation: Trace the 3 patterns to tracing paper, and cut out. Cut the following pieces from felt: 5" x 11" (12.5 x 28 cm) denim blue, 2" x 6" (5 x 15 cm) sage green, two 2" x 8" (5 x 20.5 cm) pieces of lime green, two 2" x 10" (5 x 25.5 cm) pieces of yellow, and two 9" (23 cm) squares of cranberry.

2 Fusing: Use a medium iron and a press cloth when fusing felt; never iron directly on felt. Follow manufacturer's instructions to apply fusible web to: the wrong side of the dark red cotton fabric squares, the denim blue and sage green felt pieces cut in Step 1, and 1 each of the lime green and yellow felt pieces cut in Step 1. Fuse the 2 lime green felt pieces and the 2 yellow felt pieces together.

3 Game Board: Fuse the 9" (23 cm) cranberry felt squares to the 9" (23 cm) red cotton print squares. Pin the fused squares, fabric sides together. Use the pinking shears to trim 1/8" (3 mm) from all 4 edges. Remove the pins; set aside 1 square for the game board back.

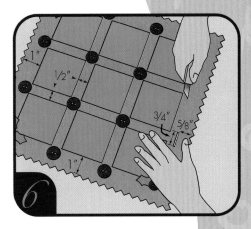

4 Blue Playing Squares: Cut nine 2" (5 cm) squares from fused blue felt. Place the squares on the cranberry felt game board front with 1/2" (1.3 cm) between the squares, and a 1" (2.5 cm) border around the outside edges. Pin, then carefully fuse squares to game board front.

5 Holly: Trace the holly leaf pattern onto the paper backing of green felt 8 times, and cut out. Refer to the photo to place 2 holly leaves in each corner, overlapping the blue squares. Fuse in place. Sew 1/2" (1.3 cm) buttons, 1 in each corner, for holly berries.

6 Buttons: Refer to the photo to sew 8 of the twelve 3/4" (2 cm) buttons between the 2 middle rows of the blue squares. Sew 2 more buttons along 1 of the outer edges. Place the remaining outer edge over a cutting surface. Refer to the Step 6 illustration to use a craft knife to make 3/4" (2 cm) slits for buttonholes at the blue square intersections, 5/8" (1.5 cm) in from the outer edge.

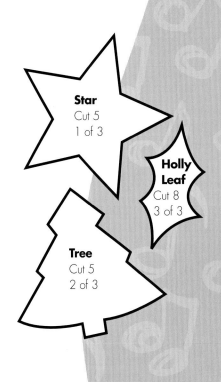

7 Game Pieces: Trace the star and tree patterns onto the fused yellow and lime green felt respectively; cut out 5 of each.

8 Blanket Stitch Border: Refer to page 155 and the Step 8 illustration for inverted blanket stitch instructions. Use 6 strands of embroidery floss in the embroidery needle to work 3/8" (1 cm) deep stitches in the pinking grooves, felt side up. Stitch along the outer edge of the gaming board front where the buttonholes were cut. Place the gaming board front on the back, fabric sides together, to find the outer edge of the gaming board back that matches the embroidered edge of the gaming board front. Work the blanket stitches on the 1 matching outer edge of the gaming board back.

9 Assembly: Pin the gaming board back and front along the unembroidered edges, fabric sides together. Embroider the front and back together with blanket stitch, as done in Step 8.

10 Storage Pocket: Use a pencil to mark the center of the buttonholes on the inside of the gaming board back. Sew remaining buttons where marked; button. Unbutton the edge to store the game pieces when not in use.

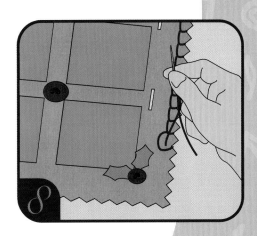

Star
Cut 5
1 of 3

Holly Leaf
Cut 8
3 of 3

Tree
Cut 5
2 of 3

Molded WAX FISH

These are the easiest fish in the world to care for! They require no food, no cleaning and no water. Best of all, they are easy and inexpensive to make— great for gifts. Melt beeswax sheets in a double boiler, and pour the wax into molds.

MATERIALS

For Both Projects
- Wicking: 2/0 for ornaments, 60 ply for candle*
- Candle mold release spray* (optional)
- Double boiler
- 8½" x 16¾" (21.8 x 42.4 cm) beeswax sheets*: 2 red and 1 each green and white for candles, 1 each yellow, red, green and white for ornaments (each sheet will make 4 ornaments)
- Candy thermometer
- Pouring pot with a spout and handle, or Pyrex® measuring cup with spout

For Candles
- Butterfly fish candle mold 3¾" x 3½" (9.5 x 9 cm)*

For Each Ornament
- Bass and sunfish candle molds*
- 6" (15 cm) gold or silver metallic cord
- White pearlizer*
- Miscellaneous items: freezer paper, apron, large-eyed darning needle, large bobby pin, scissors, stove, artist's paintbrush
- *(See Sources on page 159 for purchasing information.)

1 Preparation: Cover work area with freezer paper, wax side up. For safety, set up separate wax melting and wax pouring areas. Cut 5" (12.5 cm) cords for ornament hanging loops. Place 2 large rubber bands around the candle mold. If desired, spray candle mold release spray in mold.

2 Wicking: Thread wicking through a large-eyed darning needle; do not cut. Insert the needle through the bottom of the mold in the wicking hole, pulling T-pin inside of the mold out. Pull wick up so it extends at least 1" (2.5 cm) above candle; hold in the center of the mold with a large bobby pin, as shown in the Step 2 illustration. Leave wicking hanging out the bottom so you do not have to rethread with each new candle.

3 Melting: Place wax in the top of double boiler; place water in the bottom of double boiler. Place on stovetop burner and turn heat to medium. **Do not leave wax unattended; it is highly flammable.** The wax will take 15-25 min. to melt. Make sure the bottom pan always has water in it. Place candy thermometer in beeswax and heat to 150°-160°F (65-70°C).

4 Pouring: You will need to work rapidly during this step with the ornaments because the wax will start to harden quickly. Turn heat off; pour wax from double boiler to pouring pot. Pour into candle mold up to the top; straighten wick if necessary. Pour a little into ornament mold, place in hanging loop, and pour in more wax until level with top of mold; see the Step 4 illustration.

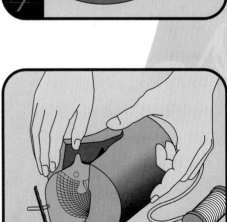

5 Unmolding: Follow manufacturer's recommended hardening times. If you will make more than 1 ornament, you may remove each after 15 min. The wax will still be slightly warm and pliable, so be careful not to make fingerprints. Remove the rubber bands from the candle mold, and gently split. See the Step 5 illustration to work the candle out. When it is all out, trim the wick flush with the bottom of the candle.

6 Candles: Melt 2 sheets of cinnamon for the red candle and 1 sheet each of jade green and white together for the turquoise candle.

7 Ornaments: See Step 6 above for the turquoise bass and sunfish; use silver cord. Melt cinnamon for the red sunfish, and sunflower for the yellow bass; use gold cord. Melt jade green for the blue fish; use silver cord. Use paintbrush and apply white pearlizer to the blue fish when cool for a sparkly, translucent finish.

APPLIQUÉD
Holly Pantsuit

Everyone likes to be dressy, yet comfortable, for the Holidays, especially when attending events with lots of good food. Nothing could be better than this holly pantsuit. The leaves are elegant green satin appliqués, accented with a plaid bow and scattered gold beads—all done on a stretchy knit tunic top and pants.

MATERIALS

- Ivory cotton knit pantsuit
- 45" (115 cm) fabrics, ¼ yd. (0.25 m) each: green satin; red Christmas plaid
- 1 yd. (0.95 m) fusible web
- Tear-away stabilizer
- Sewing threads: green, red, ivory
- Twenty-eight 6 mm gold beads
- Pattern Sheet
- Miscellaneous items: tracing and transfer paper, pencil, scissors, iron, safety pins, sewing needle, sewing machine with zigzag stitch

1 Patterns: Wash and dry cotton knit pantsuit and fabrics; do not use fabric softener. Follow manufacturer's instructions to iron fabrics, and then apply fusible web to wrong side of fabrics. Trace the patterns to tracing paper and cut out. Trace the patterns to paper backing of appropriate fused fabrics, **making sure to reverse the pattern pieces.** Make 1 each of bow and ribbons and 25 leaves. Cut out and remove paper backings.

2 Fusing: Refer to the photo to fuse 3 leaves to the bottom of each sleeve and pants leg. On shirt front, fuse bow and 3 ribbons as shown in the Step 2 illustration and then the 13 remaining leaves, overlapping as desired, in wreath shape.

3 Appliquéing: Pin tear-away stabilizer inside shirt under fused appliqués. Set the sewing machine for a closely spaced, medium-width zigzag, or satin, stitch. Loosen the needle thread tension, if necessary, so bobbin thread won't show on the right side of the fabric. Stitch so the zigzag is halfway between the appliqué pieces and the fabric. Satin stitch the bow, then ribbons, with the matching red thread; stitch holly leaves with green thread. Read Steps 4 - 7 for how to appliqué curves, points and corners. Remove stabilizer and trim threads.

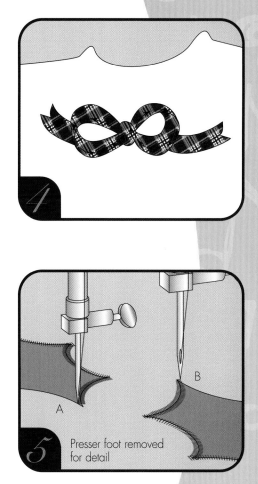

4 Appliquéing Ribbon, Leaf and Bow Curves: Pivot the fabric frequently, pivoting with the needle down at the longest edge of satin stitching. Refer to the Step 4 illustration to stitch the bow following the arrows; stitch the center knot, then the loops as shown, then any undone lines.

5 Appliquéing Ribbon, Leaf and Bow Points: Stitch, stopping when the inner edge of stitching meets the opposite side of the appliqué, as shown in illustration 5A. Pivot fabric slightly; continue stitching, gradually narrowing stitch width to 0 and stopping at the point. See 5B to pivot fabric around, and stitch back over previous stitches, gradually widening the satin stitch to its original width. Pivot fabric slightly, and stitch the next side of the appliqué.

6 Appliquéing Ribbon Inside Corners: Stitch past the corner a distance equal to the width of the satin stitches, stopping with the needle down at the inner edge of stitching. Raise presser foot, pivot and stitch the next side, covering the previous stitches at the corner.

7 Beads: Refer to the photo to hand-sew gold beads with ivory thread. Sew 3 beads for berries on each holly cluster at sleeve and pants cuffs. Sew remaining beads randomly around the wreath.

STAR
Santas

It's Christmastime! Have fun making these winsome Santas just in the "nick" of time! Using fabric scraps, you can make an entire galaxy and even get to keep a few for yourself. For a great party idea, nestle several Santas on the branches of a small tree in your entryway, then pin one to each guest's coat as he or she leaves.

MATERIALS

For Each Santa
- Cotton fabrics: 5″ x 10″ (12.5 x 25.5 cm) Christmas print; 2″ (5 cm) square muslin or brown broadcloth for face
- 12″ (30.5 cm) yarn for beard
- Polyester fiberfill, small amount
- Acrylic paints: black, white
- Liquid fray preventer
- White craft glue

For Pin
- 5 mm pom-pom for hat tassel
- 2 black seed beads
- Clear nylon thread
- ¾″ (2 cm) pin back

For Ornament
- 15 mm gold bead or jewelry bead cap
- 12″ (30.5 cm) metallic gold thread for hanger
- Miscellaneous items: ballpoint pen, tracing paper, scissors, knitting needle, tweezers, nickel, dime, toothpick, powdered blush, cotton swab, straight pin, sewing machine and matching sewing threads, sewing needle

1 Preparation: Trace the pin or ornament pattern to tracing paper. Fold Christmas print fabric in half widthwise, right sides together. Trace pattern onto fabric using the ballpoint pen; **do not cut out.**

2 Santa Star: Sew fabric layers together along pen outline, as shown in the Step 2A illustration. Cut out just beyond stitching; clip corners and curves. Refer to the pattern to carefully slit 1 fabric layer on the back. Seal raw edges with liquid fray preventer and let dry; see 2B. Use the tweezers to turn, pushing out points with knitting needle. Stuff firmly with fiberfill and slipstitch opening shut.

3 Face: Trace around a dime for the pin, or a nickel for the ornament, onto muslin or broadcloth. Cut out circle, then cut circle in half. Refer to the pattern to glue semicircle face on star body; let dry. Use the toothpick and black paint to dot eyes. Add white eye highlights with the straight pin. Blush cheeks with a cotton swab.

4 Beard: Cut yarn into 1³⁄₄" (4.5 cm) lengths and separate strands. Refer to the photo and the Step 4 illustration to glue strands on sides and lower face for hair and beard; trim. Also glue a strand to bottom of cap for fur trim.

5 Pin: Glue 2 black seed beads down center front of Santa for buttons and pom-pom tassel to hat. Use nylon thread to sew pin back to back of body.

6 Ornament: Glue gold bead or jewelry bead cap to tip of hat. Sew gold metallic thread through top center of ornament back; knot ends together for hanger, and trim.

Face

Slit back only

Star Santas
Pin
Trace to doubled fabric
1 of 2

Face

Slit back only

Star Santas
Ornament
Trace to doubled fabric
2 of 2

Good things come in small packages and these stitched jeweled boxes are so pretty that they could be elegant gifts even without something tucked inside! The braided binding stitch is a unique way to join pieces of canvas that at the same time gives a decorative finished look.

MATERIALS

For Each Box
- No. 16 tapestry needle
- White felt, 3" (7.5 cm) square

For Square Box
- 7-mesh plastic canvas, 1/3 sheet
- 14 yd. (12.88 m) ivory worsted-weight yarn
- Metallic plastic canvas yarn: 3 yd. (2.75 m) silver, 4 yd. (3.7 m) blue
- 18 mm faceted ruby heart jewel
- 11 mm antique white pearl round cabochons, four

For Round Box
- 7-mesh plastic canvas, 1/4 sheet
- 3" (7.5 cm) plastic canvas circles with spokes radiating from center, two
- 4 yd. (3.7 m) ivory worsted-weight yarn
- Metallic plastic canvas yarn: 5 yd. (4.6 m) gold, 6 yd. (5.5 m) red
- Acrylic beads: 11 mm red tri-bead; three 19 x 10.5 mm emerald holly leaves
- Miscellaneous items: scissors, white craft glue, ruler, emery board

1 General: Refer to the Plastic Canvas Instructions and Stitches on page 158. Follow the bold outline on the Stitch Charts to cut each design. Cut up to, but not into, the edge bars. Each line on the graph represents 1 bar of plastic canvas. If desired, cut a small piece of felt to line inside bottom of boxes.

2 Square Box: Cut plastic canvas as follows: one 14x14-bar piece for bottom (left unstitched); one 16x16-bar piece for lid; four 16x4-bar pieces for lid sides; four 16x11-bar pieces for box sides. Use the Gobelin stitch to work the box and lid sides following the Stitch Charts. For the lid, use the long straight stitch to work the blue and silver stitches and the continental stitch to fill in the corners. Use ivory yarn to assemble the box and lid with the braided binding stitch, and to overcast box and lid open edges. Refer to the photo to glue heart jewel to center of lid and a pearl cabochon in each corner.

3 Round Box: Cut the plastic canvas as follows: one 47x4-bar and one 42x10-bar piece. Trim 2 rows from outer edge of 1 circle for the lid and 3 rows from the other for the unstitched bottom. To stitch the lid, work gold long straight stitches around circle from every other outside edge hole to center. To fill in, stitch from unworked outside edge holes over 4 bars toward center. Use the Gobelin stitch on the lid and box sides following the Stitch Charts. Use ivory yarn to overcast box sides and bottom, and lid sides and lid together. Overcast the box and lid open edges with ivory yarn. Refer to the photo to center and glue tri-bead and leaves to the lid.

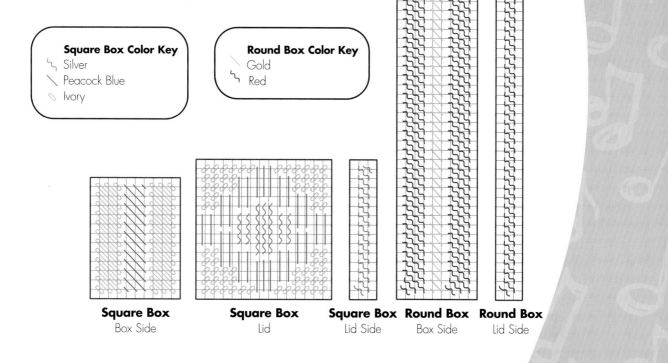

Square Box Color Key
↳ Silver
＼ Peacock Blue
✎ Ivory

Round Box Color Key
＼ Gold
↳ Red

Square Box
Box Side

Square Box
Lid

Square Box
Lid Side

Round Box
Box Side

Round Box
Lid Side

GIFT BOX STITCH CHARTS

TRIMMING *the* TREE

The Christmas tree is the focal point of the holiday celebrations, and these homemade ornaments will earn a special place on your tree year after year. From the elegant Filled Cone Ornaments to the adorable Snowman Picture Ornaments, there's something here for every style. And when the decorations are all on the tree, top it off with the Copper Angel Topper!

Angelic ANNIE

These chubby little heart-shaped angels made from country checks and homespun plaids will add a touch of warmth and whimsy to a newlywed's first apartment or a retirement complex on the beach in Florida. Angelic Annie, with those button curls and turned-in toes, finds a cozy home on an appliquéd sweatshirt or a banner, or is the perfect finishing accent to your tree and mantel.

MATERIALS

For More Than One Project
- 45" (115 cm) cotton fabrics:
  For Banner: 1/2 yd. (0.5 m) each: red check, muslin; 1/4 yd. (0.25 m) green/black check; 1/8 yd. (0.15 m) each: red/white plaid, tan/black check, and all sweatshirt fabrics
  For Tree Skirt: 1/3 yd. (0.32 m) green/black check; 1/4 yd. (0.25 m) each: red/black check, green/white plaid, red/white plaid, tea-dyed muslin, gold print, red/black check
  For Sweatshirt: 1/4 yd. (0.25 m) green/black check; 1/8 yd. (0.15 m) each: gold print, tea-dyed muslin, red/black check, green/white plaid
  For Garland (7 angels and 8 hearts): 1/4 yd. (0.25 m) each: gold print, tea-dyed muslin, red/white plaid, red/black check
- Heavy-duty fusible web: 1/2 yd. (0.5 m) each for banner and sweatshirt; 1 yd. (0.95 m) for tree skirt; 2/3 yd. (0.63 m) for garland
- Beige tortoiseshell buttons:
  7/16" (1.2 cm) large buttons: 50 for tree skirt, 5 each for banner and sweatshirt, 8 for garland
  5/16" (7.5 mm) small buttons: 8 for banner, 5 for sweatshirt, 28 for garland

- 1/4 yd. (0.25 m) red ribbon, 1/8" (3 mm) wide, each for sweatshirt and banner
- Jute twine: 29" (73.5 cm) for sweatshirt, 38" (96.5 cm) for banner, 2 1/4 yd. (2.1 m) for garland
- Black extra-fine-line permanent-ink pen
- Glues: jewelry, glue stick for garland

For 14"x 18" (35.5 x 46 cm) Banner
- 2 plastic rings, 5/8" (1.5 cm) diameter

For 50" (127 cm) Tree Skirt
- Purchased 50" (127 cm) tree skirt or 1 1/4 yd. (1.15 m) natural jute, 72" (183 cm) wide
- 6 1/2 yd. (5.95 m) natural extra-wide double-fold bias tape

For Sweatshirt
- Navy blue sweatshirt
- 1/3 yd. (0.32 m) tear-away stabilizer
- Sewing machine with zigzag stitch and matching threads
- Pattern Sheet
- Miscellaneous items: tracing and transfer paper, pencil, scissors, iron, sewing needle, tape measure, heavy brown paper, powder blush, cotton swabs, ruler, small safety pins, straight pins, string

PREPARATION

Wash, dry and iron sweatshirt and fabrics, except for jute; do not use fabric softener. Follow manufacturer's instructions to iron fusible web to wrong side of fabrics or to heavy brown paper. Trace the appropriate Large or Small Angel patterns and transfer to paper backing of fusible web. Cut out ¼" (6 mm) beyond traced lines for Sweatshirt, and on the traced lines for all other projects. Remove paper backings.

LARGE ANGEL

1 Placement: Large Angels are used on the Sweatshirt, Banner and Tree Skirt. Lay out Angel on the item; pin-mark where the top of the head and the bottom of the feet will be. Remove all the pieces, putting them back to determine placement as needed. See the illustration to fuse in the following order: wings, hands, sleeves, feet, dress, apron and head.

2 Heart Garland: Fuse red/black mini check fabric to both sides of brown paper. Transfer 5 Small Hearts to fused fabric. Cut out each heart and glue a small button to the center. Cut 13" (33 cm) of jute twine. Center and glue hearts ½" (1.3 cm) apart on jute, as shown in the illustration. Place heart garland on angel with ends hanging over hands. Cut two 8" (20.5) pieces of jute, and tie each into a small bow. Tie 1 end of garland around each bow; knot tightly and trim excess. Use small safety pins to pin garland to hands from back side.

BANNER

1 Cut a 15" x 19" (38 x 48.5 cm) banner front on the diagonal from red check, and a matching back from muslin. Follow the Large Angel instructions to fuse angel to banner front, 2½" (6.5 cm) from the banner bottom. Refer to photo to place "MY ♥ I GIVE THEE" above Large Angel, and fuse. Glue a small button to the heart. Stitch the banner front to back, right sides together, with a ⅜" (1 cm) seam allowance. Leave 4" (10 cm) opening for turning along the bottom. Turn right side out, slipstitch opening closed, and press. Tack a plastic ring to each upper back corner for hanging.

2 Glue 5 large buttons around angel's head for the hair. Tie small red ribbon bow; glue under chin. Dot eyes and mouth with black pen, as shown in the Step 2 illustration. Use cotton swab to apply small circles of blush to cheeks. See Large Angel Step 2 to make Heart Garland.

3 Fuse green/black check to both sides of 2" x 3" (5 x 7.5 cm) of brown paper for the hanging hearts. Transfer 2 Small Hearts to green check fabric; cut out. Glue a small button to the center of each heart. Cut 9" (23 cm) of jute, and tie a small bow at the center. Glue back of green hearts to jute ends. Attach jute bow to banner with a safety pin on the back side.

LARGE ANGEL

LARGE ANGEL

BANNER

TREE SKIRT

1 If you are using a purchased tree skirt, go to Step 4. See the Step 2 illustration to fold the jute in half lengthwise, then crosswise. Tie 1 end of string to a pencil, then knot string 2" (5 cm) from the pencil. Place knot at folded corner of fabric, and position pencil at single fold edges of fabric. Holding knot firmly and keeping string taut, draw a small arc in the corner for the center opening.

2 Untie pencil from string and retie 25" (63.5 cm) from knot. Repeat to draw a large arc for the tree skirt edge, as shown in the Step 2 illustration. Cut fabric along both arcs, cutting large 1 first. Open circle, then fold in half. Cut along foldline from 1 edge to center to make back opening.

3 Pin bias tape around outer edge, back edges and center opening of tree skirt, with right sides together and raw edges matching. Stitch along the first foldline of the bias tape. Clip seam allowances around the center circle; trim corners. Press bias tape to wrong side of skirt. See the Step 3 illustration to pin the bias tape in place, mitering at the corners, and stitch.

TREE SKIRT

TREE SKIRT

4 Follow Large Angel instructions to make 4 green and 3 red large angels and 8 red/green hearts from the Small Angel dress and apron hearts. Refer to the Step 4 illustration to place a red angel centered opposite skirt back opening 1½" (3.8 cm) from bottom edge. Follow Step 1 of Large Angel to fuse, adding on the Medium Heart at the end. Place remaining angels with dresses about 10" (25.5 cm) apart, alternating colors, and fuse. Center and fuse red/green hearts between angels. Repeat Step 2 of Banner, omitting bow and Heart Garland; glue 1 large button on apron Medium Heart and red/green heart.

TREE SKIRT

SWEATSHIRT

Follow Large Angel instructions to fuse 1 angel to shirt. Cut fabric stabilizer slightly larger than angel; baste or pin to inside of sweatshirt. Use matching threads to zigzag-stitch around angel, in the same order as pieces were fused. Set the sewing machine for a closely spaced, medium-width zigzag; refer to the illustration (contrasting threads were used for illustration purposes). Loosen the needle thread tension, if necessary, so bobbin thread won't show on the right side of the fabric. When satin stitching around curves, pivot the fabric frequently, pivoting with the needle down at the longest edge of the satin stitching. Remove stabilizer, and trim threads. Repeat Step 2 of Banner, sewing on buttons and bow. Remove garland when washing shirt.

SWEATSHIRT

HEART AND ANGEL GARLAND

Fuse the 7 Small Angel pieces to brown paper. See the illustration to use the glue stick to assemble 7 angels in the following order: wings, sleeves, hands, dress, apron, feet, head and Tiny Heart. Glue 3 small buttons to head for hair and 1 to center of Tiny Heart. Finish eyes, mouth and cheeks same as in Step 2 of Banner. Fuse red/black check fabric to both sides of brown paper. Transfer 8 medium hearts to fused fabric. Cut out each heart, and glue a large button to the center of each on 1 side. Glue back side of wings of 1 angel to the center of jute twine. Glue a heart 1" (2.5 cm) from each side of angel. Repeat until all 7 angels and 8 hearts are glued. Knot each jute end to form a small loop; trim.

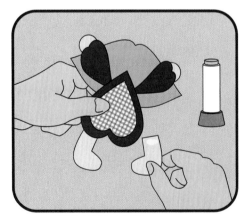

HEART AND
ANGEL GARLAND

COOKIE CUTTER *Ornaments*

The holidays bring sparkling lights and the warm glow of a fire on the hearth; what better to reflect those lights than decorations made of metal? Create these ornaments by cutting sheets of tin and copper purchased at a craft store. Nothing could be simpler or shinier!

MATERIALS

- Tin or copper sheet—a 14" x 16" (35.5 x 40.5 cm) sheet would make about 12-15 ornaments 4" (10 cm) high
- Tree and star cookie cutters (any cookie cutter will work; simple shapes work best)
- Awl and rubber mallet, tin-punching tool, or hammer and nail
- 100-grit sandpaper
- Fine steel wool
- Spray acrylic sealer
- 12" (30.5 cm) gold cord for each ornament
- 1 bead for each ornament

1 Pattern: Place tree and star cookie cutters on metal sheet. See Step 1 illustration to trace around cookie cutters with a pencil. Refer to photo to draw a zigzag line across tree to resemble a garland. Trace another star design 1/4" to 1/2" (6 mm to 1.3 cm) inside of cookie cutter line on star design. Trace all designs at one time to fill the metal sheet.

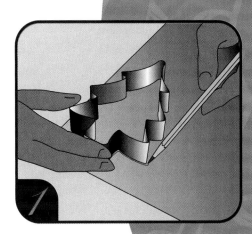

2 Hanger Hole: Place metal sheet with design area over scrap of wood. Punch hole for hanger about 1/8" (3 mm) from top edge of design. Use awl and rubber mallet, tin-punching tool, or hammer and nail.

3 Punched Design: Leave metal sheet over the scrap of wood. See the Step 3 illustration to punch holes around the star design line about 1/8" (3 mm) apart. Use the awl and mallet, tin-punching tool, or a thin nail and hammer. Punch the garland line on the tree in the same way.

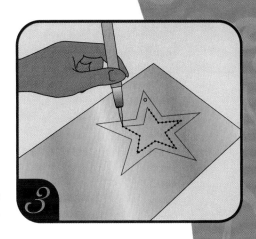

4 Cutting: Cut out star and tree along traced pencil lines with utility scissors. Trim the tips of sharp star points; gently round Christmas tree branch ends, if necessary.

5 Sanding: Lightly sand edges of ornament with 100-grit sandpaper, to smooth any rough edges. If sharp edges are raised on the back of ornament from punching, lightly hammer edges flat with rubber mallet or hammer. Do not sand the surface of the ornament if a smooth finish is desired. Rub ornament lightly with fine steel wool to remove any fingerprints; wipe clean. If a textured finish is desired, such as shown in the photo on the tin Christmas tree, rub surface lightly with sandpaper.

6 Oxidizing Surface: Sand the surface of star ornament lightly with 100-grit sandpaper. See the Step 6 illustration to hold the ornament over a flame, such as a gas stove burner, using tongs. Move ornament randomly through the flame to produce color changes. Remove from the heat occasionally to check for the desired color. Rub ornament lightly with fine steel wool to remove any fingerprints; wipe clean.

7 Hanging Loop: Spray ornament with acrylic sealer. Cut 12" (30.5 cm) of gold cord; thread through hanger hole. Hold cord ends together and string on 1 decorative bead. Knot ends of cord together, and trim. Raffia, ribbon and wire may also be used for hanging materials.

NO-TWO-ARE-ALIKE
Ornaments

These shimmery snowflakes are stitched with a variety of decorative threads—metallic braid and cord, rayon embroidery floss and needlepoint yarn—to name a few. They are then embellished with a variety of beads.

1 Preparation: Refer to the Plastic Canvas General Instructions and Stitches on page 158. Cut two 36 x 36 bar squares for each ornament. Use the Stitch Chart to cut out 2 snowflakes, a front and back. When using metallic threads, you may want to apply liquid fray preventer to the edges so they do not unravel while stitching.

2 Stitching: Follow the charts to stitch the ornaments and refer to the photo for colors. When using ribbons or braids, keep the ribbon flat, and untwisted, on the plastic canvas surface. Stitch the center design only on the snowflake front; leave the center of the snowflake back blank. Stitch the double blocks on all 8 snowflake points. Use long straight stitches for the snowflake points and center. Overcast around all edges on both snowflake pieces when done.

3 Finishing: Refer to the photo to stitch on beads as desired. Use 1 strand of matching thread or floss and the beaded half cross-stitch (or a straight stitch for bugle beads) to attach the beads to the snowflakes. When completed, place the snowflake front over the snowflake back, and gently bend the points forward and backward to snap the 2 pieces together. Use a needle to thread a 12″ (30.5 cm) hanging cord of your choice through 1 of the snowflake front points.

4 Iridescent Snowflake: Stitch a snowflake front and back with 1 strand of iridescent needlepoint yarn or braid; overcast all edges with the same. Stitch on beads as shown in photo, 2 on each snowflake point in the center of the boxes, and 5 in the snowflake front center.

5 Gold/Silver Snowflake: Use 1 strand of silver metallic cord to stitch the center design on the front and snowflake points on the back; overcast the front. Stitch the snowflake front points and overcast the back with 1 gold strand. Use gold to stitch over the 3 center stitches in each silver triangle of the snowflake front design.

6 Blue Snowflake: Use 12 strands of rayon floss to stitch the center design and snowflake points. Use 6 strands of floss for overcasting. Refer to the chart and stitch 1 snowflake front as shown. Overcast edges with med. blue floss. Stitch the snowflake back points with med. blue, and overcast with royal blue. Stitch on beads as shown in photo, 2 on 3 snowflake front points, and the snowflake charm on the remaining outer point.

7 Rainbow Snowflake: Use rainbow metallic cord to stitch the center design and snowflake points on the front; overcast with 6 strands of silver gray rayon floss. Stitch the snowflake back points with 12 strands of silver gray rayon; overcast with 1 strand of rainbow cord. Stitch on beads as shown in photo, 2 bugles on snowflake points, and 8 in the snowflake center.

SNOWFLAKE STITCH CHART

Front
Do not stitch center design on snowflake back
1 of 1

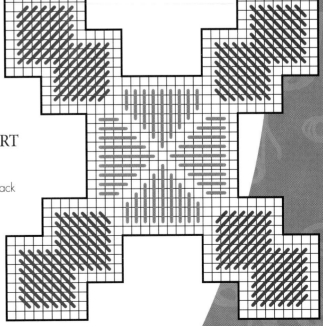

Cinnamon KIDS

Add a little spice to your tree with a family of Cinnamon Kids. Unlike their gingerbread cousins, they have an easy-to-mix, no-bake recipe that makes these kids the perfect ornaments to craft with your kids.

MATERIALS

For 6 Ornaments
- ¼ cup (50 mL) applesauce
- ½ cup (125 mL) ground cinnamon
- Six 3" (7.5 cm) squares coordinating cotton mini prints
- 3 yd. (2.75 m) coordinating ⅛" (3 mm) satin or grosgrain ribbon
- Acrylic paints: off-white, black
- Dimensional fabric paints to coordinate with fabric
- Liner paintbrush
- Spices: caraway seeds, whole cloves
- 1½ yd. (1.4 m) tan novelty loop yarn
- White craft glue
- Miscellaneous items: tracing paper, pencil, air-soluble marker, posterboard, scissors, mixing bowl, plastic cutting board, rolling pin, sharp knife, small drinking straw, spatula, paper towels, wire rack

1 Preparation: Trace the clothing patterns to tracing paper and the body pattern to posterboard. Cut out. Cut 1/8" (3 mm) satin ribbon into 12" (30.5 cm) lengths.

2 Body Dough: Place 1/4 cup (50 mL) of cinnamon in bowl. Gradually mix in applesauce. Add more cinnamon to make a doughlike consistency; lightly knead. Sprinkle a little cinnamon on cutting board and roll dough to a scant 1/4" (6 mm) thickness. Dough should yield 6 to 9 kids.

3 Bodies: Place body pattern on rolled dough and cut around it with a sharp knife; refer to Step 3 illustration. Use straw to make a hanger hole in center top of head. Cover wire rack with paper towels. Use spatula to place bodies on covered rack; let dry for 24 hours.

4 Clothes: Refer to the photo and use the air-soluble marker to trace patterns onto fabric squares. Cut 1 shirt and pants for each boy, and 1 dress for each girl. Glue to bodies. Cut 3" (7.5 cm) lengths from 12" (30.5 cm) ribbon lengths and make a coordinating ribbon bow. Glue to each girl's dress under chin. Refer to the pattern and Step 4 illustration; use dimensional fabric paints to dot buttons on each boy's shirt.

5 Faces: Dip paintbrush handle tip in off-white and dot eyes. Let dry. Repeat to add smaller black dot pupils. Refer to the pattern to freehand-paint the mouth with black.

6 Finishing: Center a 12" (30.5 cm) length of ribbon through each hanger hole and tie. Knot ends in an overhand knot. To make the hair, see the Step 6 illustration to glue caraway seeds or cloves to boys' heads, and short lengths of yarn to girls' heads.

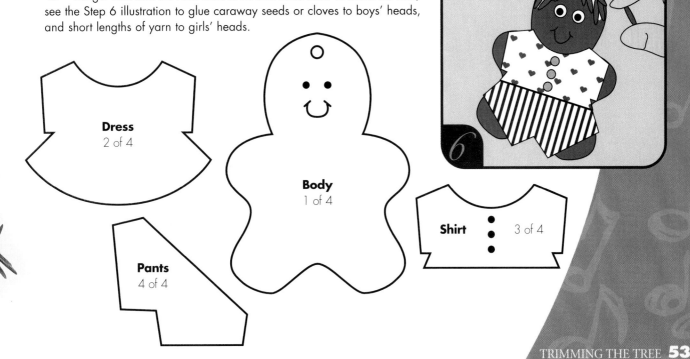

Dress
2 of 4

Body
1 of 4

Pants
4 of 4

Shirt 3 of 4

SNOWMAN
Picture Ornament

Frame your favorite family photo for the holidays in this quick-baked clay Snowman Picture Ornament. Proud grandparents or aunts and uncles would love to receive this memento to hang on their tree. Paint a date at the bottom to make it an annual collectible.

MATERIALS

- Oven-bake modeling compound: white, black, red, green
- Acrylic paints: black, white, red
- Liner paintbrush
- Gloss waterbase spray varnish
- 1/3 yd. (0.32 m) red satin ribbon, 1/4" (6 mm) wide
- 3" (7.5 cm) white felt circle
- Photo, your choice
- White craft glue
- Miscellaneous items: scissors, tracing paper, pencil, palette knife, aluminum foil, baking sheet, rolling pin, paper clip

1. Preparation: Trace the pattern onto tracing paper and cut out. Cover baking sheet with foil.

2. Snowman Body: Knead white modeling compound to a pliable consistency and use rolling pin to press to a 1/4" (6 mm) thickness. Place pattern on compound and use palette knife to cut out. Shape two 1 1/2" (3.8 cm) arms and attach 1 to each side of body as shown in the Step 2 illustration.

3. Scarf and Nose: Knead red compound and form a 1/2" x 2" (1.3 x 5 cm) piece; place on neck. Cut a 1" (2.5 cm) and 2" (5 cm) long narrow triangle. Refer to the photo to place 2" (5 cm) triangle over shoulder, following curve of the arm. Place short triangle on top and press both firmly into neck piece. Use the knife to cut fringe lines into scarf ends. Form a 1/4" (6 mm) red ball for the nose and press to center of face.

4. Holly: Knead a small piece of green and shape into two 1/2" (1.3 cm) balls. Press each ball flat and pinch ends to form holly leaves. Form 3 tiny red balls for berries. Press leaves and berries to front of snowman below left arm. Use the knife to make leaf vein lines.

5. Hat: Knead black compound and shape a 1" (2.5 cm) triangle, 1/4" (6 mm) thick for crown top. Bend paper clip in half and refer to the Step 5 illustration to insert into crown top for the hanger. Press hat to top of head. Shape a 1/2" x 2" (1.3 x 5 cm) brim and press on front over crown.

6. Baking: Bake in oven following manufacturer's instructions. Let cool completely.

7. Painting: Refer to the pattern and photo to use liner brush to outline the eyes with black paint. Paint eyes white with black pupils. Add a white highlight to each pupil. Use red to paint the mouth and cheeks and to paint tiny "stitches" around frame opening. Let dry. Spray ornament with 2 coats of varnish; let dry.

8. Finishing: Trim photo to 1/2" (1.3 cm) larger than opening and glue to back of snowman. Glue felt circle over back of photo. Thread ribbon through hanger. Knot ends to form a hanging loop.

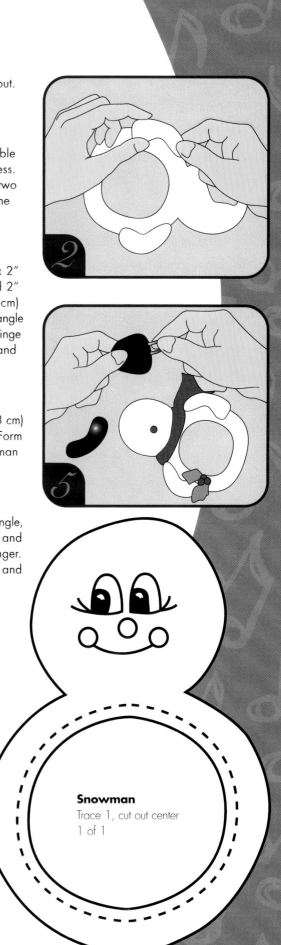

Snowman
Trace 1, cut out center
1 of 1

FILLED CONE
Ornaments

Although these cones aren't filled with ice cream, they look scrumptious enough to eat. Different style containers are decorated with dried florals and embellished with elegant ribbons—a treat for your own tree, or a gift for a special friend.

PREPARATION

See the Preparation illustration to cut triangles from foam to shape a cone to fit inside of container. Push foam so it is 1" (2.5 cm) below the top edge of the cone; secure with a few dots of hot glue. Loosely cover the top of the foam with Spanish moss; hold in place with hot glue. Hot-glue the stems of dried florals, and gently work them into the floral foam, because they can be fragile.

MATERIALS

For Each Cone
- 2½" (6.5 cm) cube dried floral foam
- Spanish moss
- Hot glue gun
- 2 wooden picks (not needed for Metal Cone)
- Floral wire

For Metal Cone
- 6" (15 cm) long, 1½" (3.8 cm) diameter metal cone container with 2 hanging loops
- 8-10 sprigs dried lavender and 5-6 sprigs green hydrangea
- 24" (61 cm) of sheer purple ribbon, 1" (2.5 cm) wide

For Gold Cone
- 5½" (14 cm) long, 2½" (6.5 cm) diameter gold plastic molded container
- 4-5 dried hydrangea sprigs, 4 pepperberry stems, 3 red and 1 gold sprigs seeded eucalyptus pods
- 1 yd. (0.95 m) of sheer gold ribbon, 1" (2.5 cm) wide

For Bark Cones
- 5" (12.5 cm) long, 2½" (6.5 cm) diameter green mushroom bark cone containers, 2
- Sheer Ribbon Cone: 4 dried rosebuds; 5 sprigs of preserved cedar; 3 each red pods and yarrow sprigs; 1 yd. (0.95 m) of sheer red ribbon, 1" (2.5 cm) wide; 8" (20.5 cm) red satin ribbon, ⅛" (3 mm) wide
- Thin Ribbon Cone: 6 dried rosebuds, 3 sprigs red yarrow; 2 sprigs seeded eucalyptus pods and 5 leaves; 4 sprigs preserved cedar; 1 sprig each red and gold pepperberries; 1 yd. (0.95 m) red satin ribbon, ⅛" (3 mm) wide
- Miscellaneous items: serrated knife, scissors, ruler

METAL CONE

Hold lavender stalks in your hand with the heads uneven. Wire them together 2" (5 cm) below the flower heads; make sure not to wrap so tight as to break the stems. Hot-glue the lavender stems and push them into the floral foam. Hot-glue hydrangea blossoms around the lavender. Cut 10" (25.5 cm) of the ribbon and tie each end to a hanging loop. Wrap remaining ribbon around the cone, and tie into a 4-loop bow.

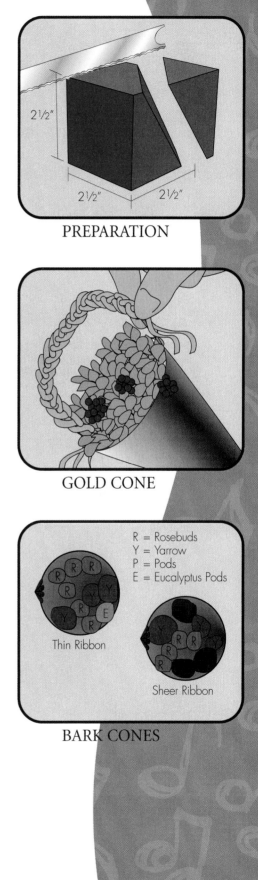

PREPARATION

GOLD CONE

1 Florals: Refer to the photo to hot-glue the stems of the dried florals and push them into the floral foam. Begin with the hydrangea sprigs, and then add the pepperberries in a diagonal from upper left to lower right. Add the eucalyptus pods to the front.

2 Handle: Cut gold ribbon into 3 equal pieces; braid, leaving 2" (5 cm) at each end. See the Gold Cone illustration to wire the end of the ribbon braid to a floral pick, leaving the ribbon ends for streamers. Hot-glue the pick, and push into the floral foam on each side of the foam as desired, to form the ornament hanging loop.

GOLD CONE

BARK CONES

1 Florals: Follow the Bark Cones illustration to hot-glue the stems of the dried florals and push them into the floral foam. Begin with the rosebuds; add the yarrow and pods. Glue the pepperberries in the center of the Thin Ribbon Cone and place the preserved cedar and eucalyptus leaves and pods around the edges of both cones.

R = Rosebuds
Y = Yarrow
P = Pods
E = Eucalyptus Pods

Thin Ribbon

Sheer Ribbon

BARK CONES

2 Handle: See the Gold Cone illustration and instructions to form the ornament hanging loop from the red sheer ribbon and red satin ribbon. Make a small, multiloop bow from the 8" (20.5 cm) red satin ribbon around 1 of the picks on the Sheer Ribbon cone.

SPOOL & CANDLE CUP *Santa*

Like the spoolie dolls we've come to love, this Santa is as easy as 1-2-3. He is made from spools, beads and candle cups strung on twine. And although he may be bald on top, he sports a fringe muslin beard that's very hairy.

MATERIALS

- Wood shapes: six ⁷⁄₈" x 1¹⁄₈" (2.2 x 2.8 cm) spools, two 1¹⁄₂" (3.8 cm) candle cups, four ¹⁄₂" (1.3 cm) round beads
- Acrylic paints: dark red, black, peach
- Paintbrushes: Nos. 4 and 12 flat
- Waterbase satin varnish
- 3" x 12" (7.5 x 30.5 cm) unbleached muslin
- 1 yd. (0.95 m) jute twine
- Glues: white craft, hot glue gun
- Miscellaneous items: heavy wire or hanger, toothpick, scissors, ruler, tea bags, water container, sewing needle, matching thread, sewing machine (optional)

1 Painting: String spools and beads on wire or hanger. Use appropriate-size brush to paint the beads black and 1 candle cup peach for the head. Paint the spools and remaining candle cup red for the body.

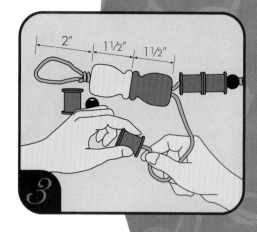

2 Face: Turn peach candle cup upside down. See page 157 for dry-brushing technique and apply red blush on cheeks. Use toothpick to dot eyes black. Let dry. Apply satin varnish to all wood pieces.

3 Head, Body and Legs: Cut 20″ (51 cm) of jute twine and fold in half. For easier threading, dip jute ends in white glue, roll to a point and let dry. Insert folded end up through hole in head. Knot above head, 2″ (5 cm) from fold, to form hanging loop. See the Step 3 illustration to thread loose ends down through body. For each leg, thread a jute end through 2 spools and a bead. Knot ends, and trim.

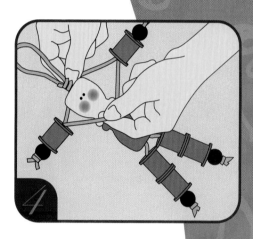

4 Arms: Cut two 8″ (20.5 cm) lengths of jute twine; align and knot at 1 end. Prepare ends for threading as in Step 3. Thread loose ends through a bead, 2 spools and another bead. Separate strands at center between the 2 spools and slip over narrow part of red candle cup, as shown in the Step 4 illustration. Pull twine tight, knot ends, and trim.

5 Beard: Fold muslin strip crosswise into thirds to make a 3″x 4″ (7.5 x 10 cm) rectangle. See the Step 5 illustration to stitch lengthwise down center of layers. On each side of seam, cut ¼″ (6 mm) strips to within ¼″ (6 mm) from center. Soak beard in a strong tea solution to dye. Let dry. Cut into two 2″ (5 cm) lengths, fold in half, and glue to face, 1 layer above the other.

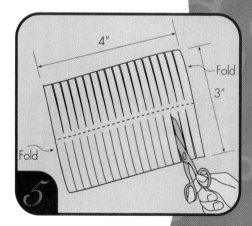

Crocheted BELLS

A

B

Crochet these delicate bells to ring in the holidays. They will look great hanging on a Christmas tree or adorning a garland of greens. A pearl bead is the shimmering clapper, and fabric stiffener gives them true form.

1 Beginning: Refer to page 154 for Crochet Abbreviations and Stitches. Use cotton thread and No. 9 crochet hook. Begin each bell with ch 6, sl st to form ring. Follow the individual bell instructions, then for each complete Steps 2-4.

2 Hanging Loop: Attach cotton thread in top of bell, ch 12, sl st to form ring, ch 1, turn, then sc over ch to beginning. Sl st in first ch, fasten off.

3 Stiffening: Hand wash crocheted bell gently in cold water with mild detergent. Press with terry cloth towel until almost dry. Cover cardboard with plastic wrap. Make a stack of paper cups that is higher than bell; cover cups with plastic wrap. Add 1 more cup to bottom to hold plastic. Stretch bell over cup, pulling to full length. Use paintbrush to apply a liberal coat of fabric stiffener. Pin the pointed tips on bottom edges to cardboard. Allow bell to partially dry, then twist off cups. Wipe excess stiffener from plastic on cups and replace bell to dry completely. Remove from cups, and twist away plastic wrap from inside bell.

MATERIALS

For Each Bell
- No. 10 white bedspread-weight cotton thread
- No. 9 steel crochet hook
- 15 mm white pearl bead
- Fabric stiffener
- 1" (2.5 cm) paintbrush or sponge brush

For Bell B
- No. 10 iridescent white metallic thread
- Miscellaneous items: scissors, paper cups or glassware, plastic wrap, rustproof pins, terry cloth towel, 6" (15 cm) square cardboard

4 Clapper: Rnd 1: Ch 4, 7 dc in fourth ch from hook, join in top of first ch-4.
Rnd 2: Ch 3 (counts as dc), dc in same sp, 2 dc in each dc around. Join in top of first ch-3. (16 dc)
Rnd 3: Ch 3 (counts as dc), dc in each dc around. Join in top of first ch-3. Insert bead and close with sl st. Ch length of bell, leaving 4" (10 cm) of thread. Fasten off. Wind unchained thread around base of hanging loop after bell is stiffened.

BELL A

Rnd 1: Ch 4 (counts as dc, ch 1), *dc in ring, ch 1. Rep from * 10 more times. Join last ch-1 in third ch of first ch-4. (12 dc with ch-1 between)

Rnd 2: Ch 5 (counts as dc, ch 2), *dc in dc, ch 2. Rep from * 10 more times. Join last ch-2 in third ch of first ch-5. (12 dc with ch-2 between)

Rnd 3: Ch 3 (counts as dc), 2 dc in ch-2 sp, *dc in dc, 2 dc in ch-2 sp. Rep from * 10 more times. Join in top of first ch-3. (36 dc)

Rnd 4: *Ch 5, sk 2 dc, sc in next dc. Rep from * 10 more times with last lp being ch 2, dc in base of first ch-5.

Rnd 5: Ch 5 (counts as dc, ch 2), dc in same sp, ch 4, sc in next lp, ch 4, *dc, ch 2, dc in next lp, ch 4, sc in next lp, ch 4. Repeat from * around. Join last ch-4 in third ch of first ch-5.

Rnd 6: Sl st in ch-2 sp, ch 5 (counts as dc, ch 2), dc in same sp, ch 5, sc in sc, ch 5, *dc, ch 2, dc in next ch-2 sp, ch 5, sc in sc, ch 5. Repeat from * around. Join last ch-5 in third ch of first ch-5.

Rnd 7: Sl st in ch-2 sp, ch 5 (counts as dc, ch 2), dc in same sp, ch 6, *dc, ch 2, dc in next ch-2 sp, ch 6. Rep from * around. Join last ch-6 in third ch of first ch-5.

Rnd 8: Sl st in ch-2 sp, ch 5 (counts as dc, ch 2), dc in same sp, ch 4, sc in ch-6 lp, ch 4, *dc, ch 2, dc in next ch-2 sp, ch 4, sc in ch-6 lp, ch 4. Rep from * around. Join last ch-4 in third ch of first ch-5.

Rnd 9: Sl st to ch-2 sp, ch 5 (counts as dc, ch 2), dc in same sp, ch 5, sc in sc, ch 5, *dc, ch 2, dc in next ch-2 sp, ch 5, sc in sc, ch 5. Rep from * around. Join last ch-5 in third ch of first ch-5.

Rnd 10: Rep Rnd 7, chaining 7 between dc, ch 2, dc.

Rnd 11: Rep Rnd 8, chaining 5 between dc, ch 2, dc.

Rnd 12: Rep Rnd 9.

Rnd 13: Sl st to ch-2 sp, ch 7, hdc in third ch from hook, ch 2, sl st in same ch as hdc (picot made), ch 1, dc in same sp, ch 6, sc in sc, ch 6, *dc in next ch-2 sp, ch 4, hdc in third ch from hook, ch 2, sl st in base of hdc (picot made), ch 1, dc in same sp, ch 6, sc in sc, ch 6. Rep from * around. Fasten off.

BELL B

Rnds 1 and 2: Follow instructions for Bell A.

Rnd 3: Ch 4 (counts as tr), 3 tr in ch-2 sp, *tr in dc, 3 tr in ch-2 sp. Rep from * 10 more times. Join to top of first ch-4. (48 tr)

Rnd 4: *Ch 1, sk 3 tr. In next tr, work 6 tr with ch 1 between each, sk 3 tr, sc in next tr. Rep from * 5 more times. Join last ch-1 in base of first ch-1.

Rnd 5: Sl st in (ch-1, tr, ch-1, tr, ch-1, tr, ch-1). Ch 5 (counts as tr). In same sp, work 5 tr with ch 1 between each. Ch 1. *In 3rd ch-1 sp of next tr fan, work 6 tr with ch 1 between each. Ch 1. Rep from * 4 more times. Join last ch-1 in fourth ch of first ch-5.

Rnd 6: Rep Rnd 5, working ch 2 between tr fans. Join last ch-2 in fourth ch of first ch-5.

Rnd 7: Rep Rnd 5, working ch 3 between tr fans. Join last ch-3 in fourth ch of first ch-5. Fasten off.

Rnd 8: Attach metallic yarn in third ch-1 sp of any fan. Rep Rnd 5, working tr fan in second ch of ch-3 of previous rnd, and eliminating ch-1 between tr fans.

Rnd 9: Rep Rnd 6, eliminating ch-2 between tr fans. Join in fourth ch of first ch-5. Fasten off.

Rnd 10: Attach cotton thread and rep Rnd 8. Fasten off.

Rnd 11: Attach metallic yarn in any ch-1 sp. Ch 1, sc in same sp, *sc in next tr, sc in next ch-1 sp. Rep from * around. Join in first sc. Fasten off.

SPORTS *Ornaments*

Sports enthusiasts will love these whimsical ornaments made from balls. Stitch a red felt hat for the Santa tennis ball, glue tees to a golf ball for the star, and string table tennis balls that are miniature reproductions into a garland.

MATERIALS

For Santa Tennis Ball
- Tennis Ball
- 20-gauge paddle floral wire, 5" (12.5 cm)
- 3¾" (9.5 cm) square red felt
- 7" x ⅜" (18 x 1 cm) white felt
- Small white pom-pom
- Hot glue gun
- 6" (15 cm) artificial pine
- 12" (30.5 cm) red braid

For Golf Ball Star
- Golf ball, plain or with holiday message
- 8 red golf tees
- Piece of foam, at least 1" (2.5 cm) thick
- Jewelry glue or rubber cement
- 12" (30.5 cm) gold cord

For Sports Ball Garland
- 3 table tennis balls that are miniature sports balls
- 22-gauge paddle floral wire, 8" (20.5 cm)
- 2 small pieces artificial pine, 3" (7.5 cm)
- Hot glue gun
- 12" (30.5 cm) each: plaid ribbon and red braid

For All Ornaments
- Drill and bits: ⅛", 1/16"
- Needlenose pliers
- Miscellaneous items: scissors, ruler, pencil, sewing machine and matching threads

SANTA TENNIS BALL

1 Hanging Loop: Drill 2 holes with ⅛" bit, directly opposite each other, in the top and bottom of tennis ball. Insert floral wire through the ball from top to bottom. Use needlenose pliers to bend 1" (2.5 cm) of top end into a loop for hanger; insert end back into ball. See the Sports Ball Garland A illustration. Bend bottom end of wire into loop; press loop flat against ball.

2 Hat: Fold red felt square in half diagonally with right side in. Stitch 1 edge of the folded felt together in a ⅛" (3 mm) seam. Turn right side out; poke tip of hat out with a pencil. Trim bottom corner from hat, as shown in the Santa illustration; round the edges.

3 Hat Trim: Hot-glue white felt strip around bottom edge of hat; begin gluing at the seam. Trim felt strip leaving a 1/4" (6 mm) overlap. Hot-glue pom-pom to tip of hat.

4 Finishing: Hot-glue hat to top of tennis ball; refer to photo to place it at an angle next to hanging loop. Bend hat tip down and glue to side of hat. Hot-glue pine bough to bottom of ball, covering bottom wire loop. Thread red braid through hanging loop and tie a knot just above loop. Tie a knot at ribbon ends; apply a dab of glue, and trim.

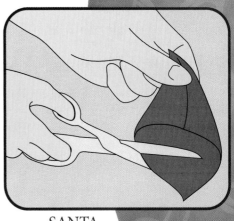

SANTA

GOLF BALL STAR

1 Hanging Loop: Drill a hole with 1/16" bit completely through a tee, 3/8" (1 cm) from the pointed end for hanging hole. Thread gold cord through hanging loop. Tie a knot at cord ends; apply a dab of glue, and trim.

2 Gluing: Insert tee with hanger into piece of foam. Apply a small drop of glue to the top of tee; place golf ball upside down on tee, pressing gently. Let glue set. Remove tee and ball from foam. Insert a second tee in the foam. See the Step 2 illustration to repeat gluing second tee directly opposite hanging loop tee. Continue gluing tees until all 8 are evenly spaced in a line around the golf ball to look like a star.

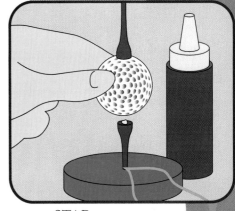

STAR

SPORTS BALL GARLAND

1 Hanging Loop: Drill 2 holes with 1/8" bit, directly opposite each other, in the top and bottom of each table tennis ball. Insert floral wire through the holes in each ball, stringing them as desired. See the Garland A illustration to use needlenose pliers to bend 1" (2.5 cm) of top end into a loop for hanger; insert end back into ball. Repeat at the other end. Wind 2 pieces of garland around wire between the balls as shown in B; spot-glue if necessary.

GARLAND

2 Finishing: Thread red braid through hanging loop and tie a knot just above loop. Tie a knot at ribbon ends; apply a dab of glue, and trim. Cut plaid ribbon into 2 pieces. Refer to photo to tie ribbons into bows through the wire loops at each end; make V cuts in bow streamer ends.

HEAVENLY *Ornaments*

The heavens provide the inspiration for these star and angel ornaments, but you'll also say "thank heavens" for how easy they are to make. A premade lace angel and yo yo speeds up the angel ornament, while wrapping floss around a coffee can lid is easy enough for even the youngest of children.

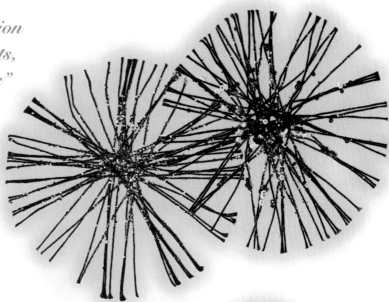

MATERIALS

For Each Star Ornament
- 1 skein embroidery floss
- Thread or fabric stiffener
- Assorted trims: glitter, seed beads
- Sponge brush or small flat paintbrush
- 4½" (11.5 cm) plastic lid (coffee can)

For Angel Ornament
- 4" (10 cm) Battenberg lace angel*
- 1" (2.5 cm) premade Christmas yo yo*
- 9" x 12" (23 x 30.5 cm) burgundy felt sheet
- Off-white embroidery floss
- ¼ yd. (0.25 m) gold metallic ribbon, ⅛" (3 mm) wide
- 8" (20.5 cm) square polyester batting
- Miscellaneous items: white craft glue, scissors, ruler, embroidery needle, straight pins, pencil, tracing paper, masking tape
- *(See Sources on page 159 for purchasing information.)

STAR ORNAMENTS

1 Cut off two 12″ (30.5 cm) pieces of floss for hangers. Wrap the rest of the skein around plastic lid, crisscrossing and distributing floss evenly. Tape end of floss on 1 side.

2 See the illustration to apply stiffener with sponge brush on 1 side, saturating all thread layers. Work over a sink or a bowl. While floss is still wet, sprinkle with glitter and beads. Let dry for manufacturer's recommended time.

STAR ORNAMENT

3 Remove tape and repeat Step 2 for other side of ornament. Carefully cut around the lid edges, forming 2 star ornaments. Trim ends if necessary. Thread each hanger piece through the ornament centers; knot ends.

ANGEL ORNAMENT

1 Trace the pattern, and cut out as indicated. Sandwich and pin batting between 2 felt hearts. See Embroidery Stitches on page 155 to blanket-stitch the heart layers together using 6 strands of floss.

2 Glue the angel to front of heart and yo yo over angel's hands. Tie a small bow from gold ribbon, and glue at neck. Thread a 6″ (15 cm) length of floss through top center of heart for the hanger; knot ends.

Angel
Heart Background
Cut 2 from burgundy felt, 1 from batting
1 of 1

Place on fold

CLOTHESPIN *Cuties*

Fans of Santa's favorite flier will delight in making these reindeer from wood spring-type clothespins and googly eyes. The tree, made from an old-fashioned clothespin covered with artificial pine, is equally charming and easy to make.

MATERIALS

For Both Projects
- Brown wood stain
- Small flat paintbrush
- Glues: wood, hot glue gun

For Each Reindeer
- 2 wood spring-type clothespins
- ¼ yd. (0.25 m) each red satin ribbon: straight-edge and picot edge, ¼" (6 mm) wide
- Two 7 mm wiggle eyes
- ⅜" (1 cm) red pom-pom
- 2 small silk holly leaves
- ⅜" (1 cm) gold jingle bell

For Tree
- 1 wooden round non-spring-type clothespin
- 1 wooden cutout star, 1" (2.5 cm)
- Acrylic paint, dark gold
- 13½" (34.3 cm) artificial pine roping, ¾" (2 cm) wide
- 3 assorted flat buttons, ½" (1.3 cm) wide
- Cotton fabrics: ¼" x 9" (6 mm x 23 cm) strip red/green plaid, 3" (7.5 cm) square red mini check
- 8" (20.5 cm) jute twine
- 6" (15 cm) red embroidery floss
- Miscellaneous items: scissors, ruler, soft cloth for staining, pencil, handsaw, sandpaper, wire cutters, paper towels

REINDEER

1 Body: Remove metal springs from both clothespins. See the Reindeer illustration to apply wood glue to each clothespin, flat sides together. Sandwich 1 end of straight-edge satin ribbon between clip ends; see 1A. When dry, glue the flat side areas of the handle ends together to make a V-shape, as in 1B.

2 Finishing: Brush on stain; wipe excess with soft cloth. Let dry. Refer to the photo to hot-glue eyes and pom-pom nose to reindeer. Hot-glue small holly leaves above eyes. Tie picot ribbon into small bow and hot-glue over leaves. Hot-glue jingle bell under bow.

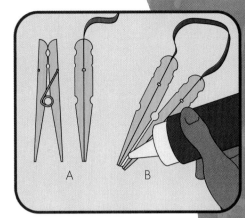

A   B

REINDEER

TREE

1 Trunk and Star: Cut 1 prong of the clothespin off with handsaw, right at and even with the base. Sand rough edges smooth. Paint the wood star dark gold; let dry. Use soft cloth to wipe stain over clothespin and painted star; wipe excess off and let dry.

2 Branches: See the Tree illustration to cut the pine roping into pieces, and hot-glue to the clothespin tree trunk. Begin 1/4" (6 mm) from the top, and leave 1/2" (1.3 cm) between the branches. When glue has set, bend branches up at ends slightly. Hot-glue star to tree top.

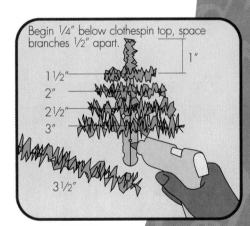

Begin 1/4" below clothespin top, space branches 1/2" apart.

1"
1 1/2"
2"
2 1/2"
3"
3 1/2"

TREE

3 Bows and Buttons: Cut red/green plaid strip into three 3" (7.5 cm) pieces. Tie a knot in the center of each piece; trim leaving 3/8" (1 cm) streamers. Hot-glue bows and buttons randomly to tree branches.

4 Tree Base: Cut a 2 1/8" (5.3 cm) circle from red mini check fabric. Hot-glue center of fabric circle to bottom of tree trunk. Wrap fabric around base. Tie red embroidery floss around fabric; knot and trim ends.

5 Hanging Loop: Tie jute twine ends together in a knot; hot-glue to back of tree trunk for hanging loop.

Clay
ANGELS

These delightful angels floating down from the heavens are easily made by pressing clay or modeling material into purchased molds that can be used over and over. After baking the clay, you paint the pieces, glue them together and hang your angels in chorus on the tree.

MATERIALS

For Each Ornament

- ½ pkg. 50 or 65 g polymer clay or modeling material:* tan or natural for Gold and Teddy Angels, red for Christmas Angel, small amount of mauve for Teddy Angel
- Artist's paintbrushes: Nos. 2 and 0 round, 2 No. 4 flat
- 12" (30.5 cm) 20-gauge gold wire or ⅛" (3 mm) satin ribbon for hanger
- 10" (25.5 cm) of 20-gauge gold wire for Gold and Teddy Angels
- Acrylic paints: metallic gold; white and peach for Gold Angel; brown, black, green, red and white for Christmas Angel; turquoise and black for Teddy Angel
- Clay push molds*: Angel Dolls and Teddy Bears
- Thick clear goopy glue
- Miscellaneous items: talcum powder or cornstarch, paint palette, water container, baking sheet, oven, scissors or craft knife, toothpicks

*(See Sources on page 159 for purchasing information.)

1 Molding: Follow manufacturer's instructions to break off small pieces of clay and warm and knead in your hands until it feels like smooth putty. Use No. 4 paintbrush to dust the inside of the mold with powder; turn mold over and tap out excess. Roll clay smaller than the area, and flatten it into the mold. Work from the center out to the edges. Use other paintbrush to brush remaining powder from clay; use scissors to trim off any excess clay.

2 Shallow and Deep Areas: See the Step 2 illustration. For shallow areas such as wings, star, feet and bows, roll a smooth ball of clay and mold, 2A. To remove, push the clay back from all edges gently and roll it up at 1 edge to lift, 2B. For deep areas such as teddy bear, balloon, angel head and dress roll a long pointed oval of clay. Mold, leaving a hunk of clay in the middle to act as a handle, 2C. To remove, push the clay back from all edges gently, and use the handle to pull the clay out, 2D.

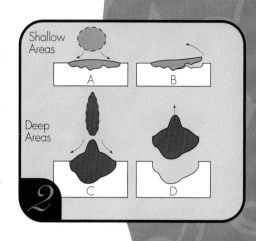

3 Baking: Cut gold wire into 5" (12.5 cm) pieces. Gently insert the wire into the balloon and stars, at least ¼" (6 mm). Be careful not to poke the wire out the front. Use a toothpick to scratch surfaces where head, dress and shoes will join. Press pieces firmly together. Bake according to clay manufacturer's instructions, usually 20-30 minutes until hardened on a baking sheet in a 265°F (132°C) oven.

4 Gold Angel: Make 1 angel head, 2 wings, 1 pair of shoes, 1 dress and 2 large stars from natural clay. Press head and shoes onto dress, and bake. Let paint dry between each color. Use the No. 2 brush to paint face, hands and feet with peach, if desired. Paint wings, all of dress, stars, shoes and hair white. Paint wings, all of dress, stars, shoes and hair lightly with metallic gold, except leave pinafore and a thin line along the stitches above dress ruffle white. Use a toothpick and gold paint to dot buttons and eyes; make mouth and bottom pinafore stitches.

5 Assembly: Take stars with gold wires, and wrap once around wrist, from back to front, referring to photo. Add a drop of glue to back of hand on wire to stabilize. Glue wings onto back of shoulders. Place a line of glue on back of head and wings. Place hanging ribbon ends in glue; layer glue over ribbon.

6 Christmas Angel: Make same as Step 4 Gold Angel except with red clay, and make a bow and only 1 large star. Paint face, hands and feet with brown; paint hair black. Use toothpick to dot eyes with white, and then black. Use the No. 0 brush to paint the mouth red. Paint bow and pinafore green. Use the No. 0 brush to paint green stitches on wings, dress, and shoes; see the Step 6 illustration to paint red stitches on the pinafore and its buttons. Paint green dots on shoe and pinafore buttons. Brush the star lightly with gold paint. Repeat Step 5 to assemble and make hanging loop, gluing large star to left hand and bow to hair.

7 Teddy Angel: Make 1 large teddy and 1 bow from tan clay. Make 2 angel wings, 1 large star and 1 balloon from mauve clay; bake all pieces. Use the No. 2 round brush to paint the ribbon turquoise; let dry. Paint all the pieces lightly with metallic gold; let dry. Use the No. 0 round brush or toothpick to dot eyes with black; paint the top paw pads, inner ears, belly button, nose and mouth with black. Repeat Step 5 to assemble and make hanging loop, gluing a star and balloon to each hand and bow to neck; see the Step 7 illustration.

Punch 'n Fold
BOXES

Punch 'n Fold Boxes
offer a '90s update
to traditional box
ornaments. Folded
white posterboard
becomes fun and
festive when trans-
formed with the
many paper punches
and trims available.

MATERIALS

- White posterboard: 6" (15 cm) square for each triangle box, 7" (18 cm) square for each star box
- Paper punches: star, teardrop, 1/4" (6 mm) round
- Trims for triangle boxes: 8" (20.5 cm) red rattail cord for each hanger and 6" (15 cm) for each side bow; 1/3 yd. (0.32 m) irides-cent cord, 3/8" (1 cm) wide for double triangle box
- Trims for star boxes: 8" (20.5 cm) white rat-tail cord or 1/16" (1.5 mm) satin ribbon for hanger; 1/3 yd. (0.32 m) pearl bead string, 2 mm wide; and 1/3 yd. (0.32 m) white satin ribbon, 1/8" (3 mm) wide for double star box
- Thick white craft glue
- Pattern Sheet
- Miscellaneous items: scissors, pencil, ruler, tracing paper, transfer paper

TRIANGLE BOX

1 Patterns: Trace the pattern to tracing paper. Transfer to the dull side of posterboard and cut out. Lightly mark placement of holes to be punched on all 3 sides. Choose from 3 different punch patterns.

2 Folding: Place ornament on flat surface, glossy side up. See the Step 2 illustration to score foldlines by holding ruler firmly along line and using scissors blade to lightly mark posterboard. Crease poster-board on scorelines toward the dull side.

3 Punching: Punch stars and teardrops where marked. To punch the center, fold over 1 side section and punch both sides together. Punch remaining side separately.

4 Hanger: Position round punch at peak of center side and punch out a half-moon shape. Cut 8″ (20.5 cm) of red rattail and knot ends in an overhand knot. Glue knot inside peak just below half-moon hole.

5 Gluing: Refer to the pattern to glue Flap A. If desired, stuff box with fabric, netting or tissue so color shows through punched holes. Glue Flaps B and C to lower sides to close bottom of box.

6 Triangle Box Variations: Cut three 6″ (15 cm) lengths of red rattail and tie each into a bow, knotting streamer ends. Glue a bow to each side of box. Or make a single bow, and glue to top of box at hanging loop base. For double triangle box, follow Steps 1-5 to make 2 boxes, omitting the hanger for 1 of the boxes. Glue bottoms together, and glue ³⁄₈″ (1 cm) cord around center to hide the seam.

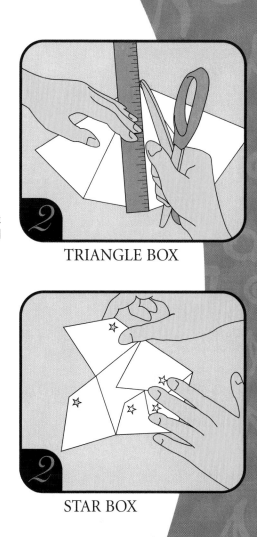

TRIANGLE BOX

STAR BOX

STAR BOX

1 Patterns, Folding and Punching: Repeat Steps 1-3 from Triangle Box, choosing from 2 different punch patterns. Punch stars or teardrops where marked.

2 Closing Box: Place on flat surface, shiny side down; see the Step 2 illustration. Working counterclockwise, fold flaps toward center, folding tip of fourth flap under first flap. Tuck the entire right edge and tip of last flap under the left edge of beginning flap.

3 Hanger: Cut 8″ (20.5 cm) of white rattail or ribbon and knot ends in an overhand knot. Glue knot to 1 point on back of box.

4 Double Star Box: Follow Steps 1-2 to make 2 boxes with the same punched pattern. Cut 8″ (20.5 cm) of ¹⁄₁₆″ (1.5 mm) ribbon. Align ends and glue to the back of 1 box point. Glue boxes together on back sides. Refer to the Step 4 illustration to glue pearl bead string around edges with ends meeting at hanger. Cut ¹⁄₈″ (3 mm) ribbon in half and tie each length into a bow. Glue a bow on each box at hanger base.

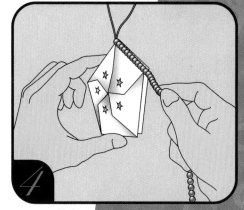

STAR BOX

FURRY FRIENDS
Photo Ornaments

If you're greeted by a wet kiss from your dog, or a cuddly cat affectionately wrapping around your ankles, then here's a way to remember the four-legged members of the family. Picture purr-fect photo ornaments are stitched on plastic canvas with embroidery floss and metallic braid.

MATERIALS

For Each Ornament
- 10-mesh plastic canvas, ¼ sheet
- 1 skein each 6-strand DMC embroidery floss: for cat ornament: Black No. 310, Lt. Steel Gray No. 318; for dog ornament: Lt. Tan No.437
- Metallic braids: 2½ yd. (2.3 m) heavy No. 32 gold; 1½ yd. (1.4 m) medium (No. 16)

red; for cat ornament only: 1½ yd. (1.4 m) heavy (No. 32) green
- No. 20 tapestry needle
- ¼ yd. (0.25 m) red satin ribbon, ⅛" (3 mm) wide
- Thick white craft glue or hot glue gun
- Miscellaneous items: scissors, craft knife, lightweight cardboard

1 Preparation: See Plastic Canvas General Instructions and Stitches on page 158. Cut one 24x43-bar piece of plastic canvas for cat ornament and one 25x43-bar piece for dog ornament; trim plastic canvas according to chart bold outlines. Stitch each ornament using 12 strands of floss or stitch 1 strand of metallic braid.

2 Cat Ornament: Work Lt. Steel Gray No. 318 continental stitches for fish body and a Black No. 310 cross-stitch for eye. Working on top of background stitches with metallic braid, make green short straight stitches for holly leaves and red French knots for berries. Overcast edges with gold metallic braid.

3 Dog Ornament: Work Lt. Tan No. 437 continental stitches to fill background. Work cross-stitches with red metallic braid on top of background stitches. Overcast edges with gold metallic braid.

4 Finishing: Mount pet photo on lightweight cardboard and glue behind opening. Tie 7" (18 cm) of red ribbon into a bow; glue to top front center. Cut 8" (20.5 cm) of gold metallic braid for the hanger. Glue ends to top back center.

CAT ORNAMENT

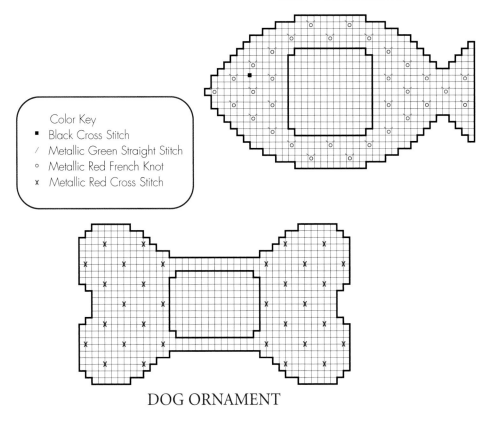

Color Key
- ■ Black Cross Stitch
- / Metallic Green Straight Stitch
- ○ Metallic Red French Knot
- × Metallic Red Cross Stitch

DOG ORNAMENT

FOLDED-RIBBON
Ornaments

You're sure to get hooked on the simple fold and pin technique used to piece this variation of a star quilt pattern. Gold beads add to the decorative design created by the points fashioned from coordinating ribbons. Quickly pin several of these ornaments to fill a basket near your front door. Share the holiday spirit by giving an ornament to friends popping in to visit or even the busy letter carrier who delivers all those wonderful Christmas greeting cards.

MATERIALS

- 3" (7.5 cm) satin balls with removable ornament caps: red, blue
- Woven double-face ribbons:
  for the red ornament: 1⅓ yd. (1.27 m) red/green plaid, 1½" (3.8 cm) wide; 1 yd. (0.95 m) each 1" (2.5 cm) green and 1½" (3.8 cm) red grosgrain;
  for the blue ornament: 1⅓ yd. (1.27 m) blue/green plaid, 1½" (3.8 cm) wide
- Gold sequin pins

- Gold beads: for red ornament: 3 mm, 48; 4 mm, 14; for the blue ornament: 3 mm, 57; 4 mm, 2
- 5 mm gold sequins (blue ornament only), 9
- 2 gold jewelry end caps, 11 x 10 mm
- 22-gauge covered floral wire, 3" (7.5 cm) for each ornament
- White craft glue
- Miscellaneous items: tape measure, scissors, wire cutters, rotary cutter and mat (optional)

RED ORNAMENT

1 Folding Star Points: Cut green grosgrain into 2" (5 cm) lengths and red grosgrain and plaid ribbons into 3" (7.5 cm) lengths. See the Step 1 illustration to fold 8 plaid star points. Fold ribbon in half widthwise to find center, then fold top corners to meet at center bottom; 1A. Fold outer folds again to meet at center; 1B.

2 Plaid Star Point Layer: Pin a 4 mm bead at center front of ornament. See the Step 2A illustration to pin 8 plaid star points, folded edges up, in a circle around 4 mm bead. Let small areas of the ball show between star points. Use sequin pins alone at outer edges where marked with white x's. At yellow dots, add 3 mm beads before pinning. Repeat on the opposite side.

3 Green Star Point Layer: See the Step 1A illustration only to fold 8 wide star points from green grosgrain. See the Step 2B illustration to pin 8 green star points, folded edges down, overlapping slightly and placing green star points between plaid points. Repeat on the opposite side.

4 Red Star Point Layer: Remove ornament cap. See the Step 1A and B illustrations to fold red ribbons into star points. See the Step 4 illustration to pin red star points, folded edges up, in a row around the ornament to cover the space between green star points, overlapping points 7/8" (2.2 cm). When pinning ribbon over cap hole, slit the ribbon between inner folds to insert hanger later. Where marked with yellow dots, add 4 mm beads to pins before pinning.

5 Hanger: Insert ends of wire through top of jewelry end cap; twist ends, leaving a 1/2" (1.3 cm) loop on top. Insert wire ends at ribbon slit and glue cap to ornament.

BLUE ORNAMENT

1 Plaid Star Layer: Cut blue plaid ribbon into sixteen 3" (7.5 cm) lengths. Repeat Red Ornament Steps 1 and 2 to fold and pin eight 3" (7.5 cm) blue star points to each side of ornament. Make sure outer points meet, and 2 points should meet at ornament cap.

2 Beading: See the Blue Ornament illustration to remove the 4 pins where points meet. Slide a 3 mm bead, then sequin, onto a single pin. Also pin at inner corners of each B ribbon. At yellow dots, slide a 3 mm bead only onto pin. Follow Red Ornament Step 5 to make a hanger.

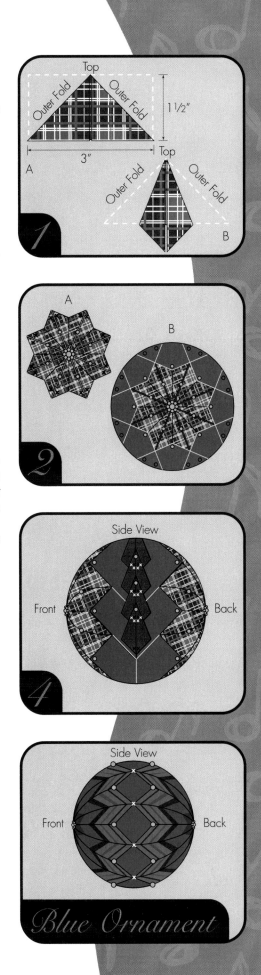

Barnyard Bell
BUDDIES

For 3 Ornaments
- 3 wooden oval cutouts, 1/4" (6 mm) thick: 2 at least 1 5/8" x 2" (4 x 5 cm), 1 at least 2" x 2 1/2" (5 x 6.5 cm)
- Scroll saw
- 3 metal jingle bells, 2 1/2" (6.5 cm) wide
- 3 wooden heart cutouts: one 1/8" (3 mm) thick, two 1/2" (1.3 cm) thick
- Paintbrushes: No. 4 flat, fine liner
- Acrylic paints: black, white, mauve
- Clear acrylic spray
- Satin ribbon, 1/8" (3 mm) thick: 2/3 yd. (0.63 m) pink, 1 1/3 yd. (1.27 m) red
- Excelsior
- Hot glue gun
- 3 gold cow bells, 1/2" (1.3 cm) wide
- Miscellaneous items: pencil, tracing and graphite paper, scissors, stylus, ruler, sandpaper, tack cloth

Decorate the branches of your Christmas tree with handmade ornaments full of animal-lover appeal. You might want to hum "Jingle Bells" while you are painting the whimsical lamb, cow and pig; only a few times through that tune with paintbrush and hot glue gun in hand will finish off this trio.

1 Preparation: See page 156 for Painting Instructions and Techniques. Trace head patterns to tracing paper, and cut out. Trace head outlines only onto the appropriate wooden oval cutouts; use scroll saw to cut out. Sand lightly; remove sanding dust with tack cloth.

2 Basecoat: Use the No 4. flat brush to basecoat each large jingle bell body with 2 coats of paint; paint 2 bells white and 1 bell pink. Create a pink color by mixing white with mauve. Basecoat cow and lamb heads on both sides and edges with white, and pig head with pink. Basecoat 2 thick wooden heart cutouts with black, and the thin 1 with mauve.

3 Spots: Paint 1" (2.5 cm) irregular black spots with the No. 4 flat brush on the jingle bell cow body, 3 on the top half, and 4 on the bottom half.

4 Lamb Head: Transfer the face painting details to all 3 basecoated animal heads. When painting, extend the colors down over the edges. Use the No. 4 brush for large areas, and the fine liner for details. When paint is dry, spray each bell, head and feet with acrylic spray; let dry. Paint the lamb head black in the center and ears.

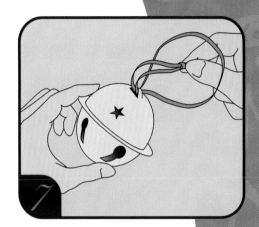

5 Pig Head: Paint ears, snout and bangs mauve. See the Step 5 illustration to use liner brush and black paint to paint pupils; to outline ears, snout and eyes; and to make nostrils, eyelashes and bangs. Highlight pupils with a white dot.

6 Cow Head: Paint ears, bangs and eye pupils black. Use the liner brush to outline the eyes and make eyelashes. Dot each pupil with a white highlight. Paint a wavy black line across face for nose. Mix white and black paint to make a light gray; paint muzzle and top of horns with gray. Paint black nostrils and mauve mouth.

7 Hanging Loop: Cut ribbon into 12" (30.5 cm) pieces. Knot both ends of 1 piece together, and thread through bell hanger. Pull knotted ends through loop, as shown in the Step 7 illustration. Pull tight to knot ribbon onto bell hanger for a hanging loop.

8 Finishing: Hot-glue heart feet to center bottom of bell body, placing point toward the back. Glue center of remaining ribbon to back side of head, so ends will hang down near mouth. Refer to the photo to glue head to jingle bell body at an angle near hanger. Thread small cow bell onto ribbon ends and tie a bow under neck. Hot-glue a small amount of excelsior around ribbon at neck.

BUDDY HEAD
PATTERNS

LAMB

PIG

COW

HANDMADE
Paper Ornaments

Here is a way to use all of that cut glass that Grandma loved so well. Press paper pulp onto the back of relish trays, the bottom of serving bowls and bases of tumblers to create beautiful patterns. Embellish with gold beads, cord, spray paint and ribbons, and you have party favors, gifts or ornaments for your tree.

MATERIALS

For Each Ornament
- 7" x 9" (18 x 32 cm) cotton linter paper*
- Gold wired-beads-by-the-yard, 3/16" (4.5 mm) diameter: 9" (23 cm) for A, 2" (5 cm) for B, 24" (61 cm) for C
- Plastic doilies
- Cut-glass items: bowls, trays, glasses, platters
- Gold spray paint
- 12" (30.5 cm) gold cord/ribbon for hanger
- Hot glue gun
- Matte spray finish or polyurethane
- 60-lb. (27 kg) drawing paper: 8" (20.5 cm) square each for A and C
- Gold cheesecloth: 6" (15 cm) square each for A and C
- Pattern Sheet
- Miscellaneous items: large mixing bowl, measuring cups, hand mixer, bath towels, fan, slotted spoon, sponge, tracing paper, pencil, soft cloth or rag, scissors

*(See Sources on page 159 for purchasing information.)

MAKING PAPER

1 Pulp: Wet the linter paper and tear it into 2" (5 cm) pieces. Soak in a large bowl or pail full of water overnight. Put 2 handfuls of pulp in a large mixing bowl, and add just enough water to cover the paper, about 2 to 3 cups (500 to 750 mL). Beat for 5 minutes at low speed with hand mixer. The pulp will fluff up and smooth out to the consistency of mashed potatoes. Add more water if mixture is too thick, and more pulp if it is too thin.

2 Molding: Lay down bath towels and set up fan in work area. Choose cut-glass item, and use slotted spoon to dust surface with pulp. You should still be able to see the glass design through the pulp. To embed cord or beads in paper, place them on the pulp now. Refer to the Step 2 illustration to continue spooning pulp until desired surface is 1/4" to 1/2" (6 mm to 1.3 cm) thick.

3 Finishing: Use the sponge to press pulp into the glass and to remove excess water, wringing frequently. Place items about 6" (15 cm) in front of fan, and dry overnight. Gently peel back paper from glass; it should feel dry and crispy. Tear or trim edges, and assemble with hot glue gun as required in individual ornament instructions. When done, spray front and back of ornaments with finish or polyurethane, following manufacturer's instructions for usage and drying times.

ORNAMENT A

1 Paper Shapes: Make a 3" (7.5 cm) circle for center on a water glass base, embedding a circle of gold beads. Make a 5" (12.5 cm) circle, embedding several gold threads or cords. Let dry; leave edges ragged. Spray gold paint on rag, and lightly rub in center circle.

2 Snowflake Background: Trace pattern to tracing paper. Fold 60-lb. (27 kg) paper square twice. Place pattern on paper, matching fold-lines. See the Step 2 illustration to cut out snowflake, and open up. Lay flat, and spray-paint both sides gold, following manufacturer's instructions for usage and drying times. Repeat with spray finish or polyurethane. Use fingers to crease the snowflake points for more dimension.

3 Assembly: Squeeze hot glue in the center of gold snowflake. Place gold hanging cord with ends in glue, and loop at desired top of ornament. Add cheesecloth square while glue is still warm; see Step 3 illustration. Apply another glue dab to the center of cheesecloth, and glue on the 5" (12.5 cm) circle; repeat to glue the center circle.

ORNAMENT B

Make a 3½" (9 cm) and 5" (12.5 cm) circle, embedding several gold threads or cords. Make an 8" (20.5 cm) circle for background on plastic doily. Spray gold paint on rag, and lightly color star design on 3½" (9 cm) circle and doily texture on background. Spray entire 5" (12.5 cm) circle gold. Repeat Step 3 Assembly of Ornament A, and cut gold trim apart with scissors into 7 beads; refer to photo to hot-glue to outer edge of center circle.

ORNAMENT C

Make a 5½" (14 cm) circle, embedding four 3" (7.5 cm) strands of gold beads evenly spaced. Let dry; leave edges ragged. Spray gold paint on rag, and lightly rub circle to highlight texture. Repeat Step 2 of Ornament A with Ornament C pattern to make snowflake background. Repeat Step 3 of Ornament A and cut gold trim apart with scissors into 7 groups of 3 beads and 6 individual beads; refer to photo to hot-glue.

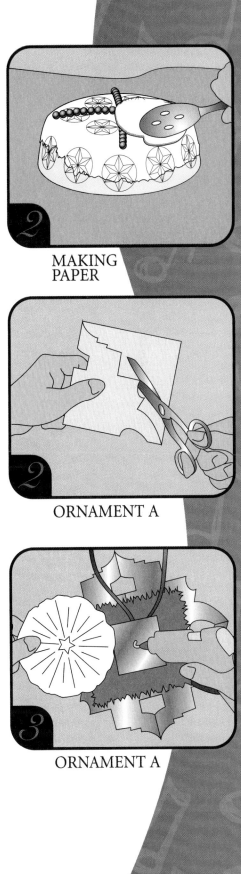

MAKING PAPER

2
ORNAMENT A

3
ORNAMENT A

Ribbon ANGELS

Need some quickie ornaments for gifts or to fill some bare spots on the tree? These angels will do the trick. Simply made from wood beads and ribbon, they would be a perfect project for the Scouts or Sunday school class, too.

MATERIALS

For Each Angel
- Red, white or green satin ribbon: 6" (15 cm) for dress, 2¼" (6 mm) wide; ½ yd. (0.5 m) for legs, ⅛" (3 mm) wide; 4" (10 cm) around neck, ¹⁄₁₆" (1.5 mm) wide.
- Metallic gold ribbon: 6½" (16.3 cm) wire edge, 1½" (3.8 cm) wide; 2" (5 cm), ¼" (6 mm) wide.
- Gold cord: 8" (20.5 cm) for hanger, 3" (7.5 cm) elastic.
- ½" (1.3 cm) gold rose
- Wood beads: one 20 mm; two 10 mm
- Acrylic paints: black; red, white or green to match ribbon
- Wavy wool doll hair, 1¼" (3.2 cm)
- ⅜" (1 cm) brass heart charm
- White craft glue or low-temp glue gun
- Miscellaneous items: scissors, ruler, large-eyed needle, toothpick, blush, cotton swab, small paintbrush, gold and matching threads, sewing machine (optional)

1 Hair Bow: Tie a small bow in center of ⅛" (3 mm) ribbon. Thread both ends through the 20 mm bead. Apply a dot of glue to secure ribbon at top of head. Pull bow down slightly into hole to make loops stand up.

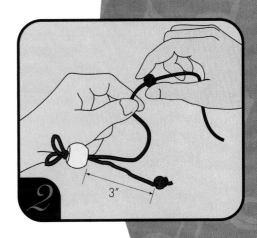

2 Legs: Paint 10 mm beads to match satin ribbon; let dry. Thread a 10 mm bead through each ribbon end, as shown in the Step 2 illustration, 3" (7.5 cm) from bottom of head; knot and trim.

3 Dress: Right sides together, sew the short ends of 2¼" (6 cm) ribbon in a ⅛" (3 mm) seam; turn right side out. Sew a gathering thread along 1 long edge. See the Step 3 illustration to place dress over legs below head bead and pull gathers tight. Knot and trim ends; apply a dot of glue at neck to hold.

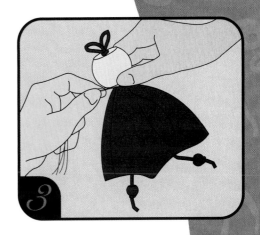

4 Wings: See Step 4A illustration to overlap ends of wire-edge ribbon at center. Use gold thread to sew down center of all 3 layers. Pull gathers tight (see 4B) and wrap around center several times; knot and trim. Glue to back of neck.

5 Head: Use toothpick to dot black eyes and cotton swab to apply blush to cheeks. Glue hair to top of head leaving bow exposed. Glue ends of elastic cord into a circle halo and glue slightly off-center to top of head.

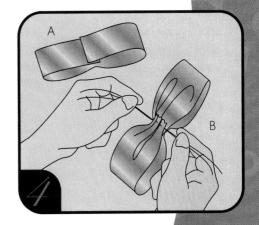

6 Finishing: For the hanger, thread gold cord in needle and run through center of hair bow. Knot ends and trim. Fold ¼" (6 mm) gold ribbon in half, cut slant ends and glue to back of rose. Glue rose to front of dress. Thread charm on 1/16" (1.5 mm) ribbon, tie a bow and glue to center front neck.

LIGHT BULB *Santas*

It's hard to believe these jolly Santas were once discarded light bulbs. Paint face, beard and hat, and just like real Santas who come in all shapes and sizes—you'll have a collection of large and small, rotund and slim characters. Even bulbs with small bases can become Santas, by adding a red felt hat and cotton batting pom-pom.

MATERIALS

- Used light bulbs
- Acrylic paints: peach, gray, berry red, Christmas red, napa red, black, white
- Textured snow paint
- Paintbrushes: Nos. 2, 4, 10 flat; No. 1 liner
- Matte acrylic spray
- Satin waterbase varnish
- 9" x 12" (23 x 30.5 cm) red felt sheet
- 10" (25.5 cm) gold cord or red ribbon for each hanger
- White craft glue
- Miscellaneous items: tracing paper, graphite paper, pencil, disposable palette, water container, small piece of cotton batting or cotton balls

1 Preparation: See page 156 for Painting Instructions and Techniques. Mist each bulb with several light coats of acrylic spray to prepare surface for painting. Use the No. 4 brush to paint the bulb base with 2 coats of Christmas red. Basecoat face area with 2 coats of peach.

2 Face: Trace the desired face pattern and transfer to bulb or lightly sketch freehand with a pencil. Use No. 2 and liner brushes to paint face details. Use a berry red wash to blush cheeks. Paint the nose berry red; outline with napa red. Paint eyes black, and eyebrows if appropriate. Paint white highlights on eyes, top of nose and cheeks, referring to photo and pattern.

3 Beard: See the Step 3 illustration to basecoat remainder of bulb with No. 10 brush and gray paint. Use vertical strokes to resemble beard and hair; then overstroke with white. Paint mustache and eyebrows, where appropriate, white. Paint the mouth napa red.

4 Painted Hat Santa: Glue a gold cord hanger to top of ornament. Refer to the photo and pat textured snow paint around bottom of hat for fur and on top for the tassel. Apply 2 coats of varnish to ornament.

5 Felt Hat Santa: Trace the hat pattern and cut from felt. With right sides together, glue seam. Turn right side out and glue hat on head. Cut a hatband and tassel from cotton batting and glue on hat. Glue hat tip to side of hat as shown in illustration. Tie a red ribbon loop through hat. Apply 2 coats of varnish to bulb only on ornament.

Face Patterns

Hat
Cut 1 from red felt

Place on fold

BUTTON & BEAD *Ornaments*

Pull out your stash of buttons and beads. Arrange them on foam and hold in place with sequin pins. No one will ever guess these ornaments took only minutes to make.

MATERIALS

For All Ornaments
- Styrofoam® shapes: 3" (7.5 cm) ball; 11" x 12" x ½" (28 x 30.5 x 1.3 cm) block, 3 stars, ½" x 4" (1.3 x 10 cm)
- 1" (2.5 cm) sponge brush
- Sequin pins: ¾" (2 cm) gold for ball; ½" (1.3 cm) gold for heart and wreath, ½" and ¾" (1.3 and 2 cm) silver for stars, Size 17 1¹¹⁄₁₆" (2.7 cm) steel silk pins for stars
- Thick white craft glue

For Button Ornaments
- Pink acrylic paint
- White and pearl flat buttons, assorted sizes
- Pink pearl seed beads
- ½" (1.3 cm) white gimp braid, ½ yd. (0.5 m) each for heart and wreath
- Gold cord, 10" (25.5 cm) for each ornament
- 1½" (3.8 cm) pink sheer ribbon, ½ yd. (0.5 m) for each ornament

- Pattern Sheet

For 3 Star Ornaments
- Ultra-fine iridescent glitter
- Opaque crystal beads: fifteen ¼" (6 mm) bugle beads, twenty ½" (1.3 cm) bugle beads, five 6 mm round faceted, twenty-five 6 mm faceted spacer
- Crystal beads: six 10 mm round faceted, 15 each 8 mm and 10 mm round faceted, 10 each 6 mm oval and 18 mm faceted spaghetti, 30 rocaille, 51 seed, twenty 6 mm faceted spacer
- Clear round rhinestones: thirty-five 5 mm, two 7 mm
- 1 yd. (0.95 m) clear monofilament for hangers
- Miscellaneous items: pencil, scissors, tape measure, tracing paper, craft knife, disposable palette, darning needle, wax paper, toothpicks

BUTTON ORNAMENTS

1 Ornament Base: Trace the heart and wreath patterns to tracing paper; trace onto foam block. Use the craft or a serrated knife with a sawing motion to cut heart and wreath from foam. Paint foam bases pink, on front, back and edges.

2 Decorating: Place 1 seed bead on each pin; dip pin into craft glue and push through buttonhole into foam. See the illustration to use 2 pins for each button. Cover entire ball and front side only of heart and wreath. Refer to the photo to alternate button sizes. Use smaller buttons to fill in or add a few beaded pins to exposed areas.

3 Finishing: Glue braid to outer and inner edges of heart and wreath, overlapping ends at center top. Use the darning needle to make a small hole in ball ornament and at center top edge of heart and wreath. Squeeze glue in hole, then press gold cord ends inside hole for hanger. Tie a pink ribbon bow, and glue to center top of ornament.

BUTTON
ORNAMENTS

STAR ORNAMENTS

1 Ornament Base: Place stars on wax paper, and use paintbrush to apply thinned white craft glue to all star surfaces. Sprinkle with glitter and let dry.

2 Decorating: Refer to the photo to decorate glitter-covered stars with beads and rhinestones. See the Star Ornament illustration to thread beads on pins, dip in craft glue before inserting into foam. Use the Size 17 steel silk pins for beaded design along the star edges, and the sequin pins for beaded design on the star fronts. Glue rhinestones and beads on star fronts to complete design.

3 Finishing: Use needle to make a hole from 1 side to the other through 1 star point, 1/2" (1.3 cm) in from the edge. Thread 12" (30.5 cm) of monofilament through the hole, knot ends and trim.

STAR
ORNAMENTS

COPPER
Angel Topper

Listen closely; you can almost hear the trumpet sound! Floating on high, this gleaming beauty will make any Christmas tree heavenly, but she can also be used as a table centerpiece or nestled in a plant. To make the angel from a sheet of copper, trace the design lines from front and back to emboss and texture with a screwdriver and marker. Her patina comes from India ink or shoe polish.

MATERIALS

- 12" x 18" (30.5 x 46 cm) mediumweight copper
- Black steel-tipped pen and marker
- India ink or black shoe polish
- 1½" (3.8 cm) copper pipe, ¾" (2 cm) diameter
- Drill and 11/64" bit
- 1¼" (3.2 cm) machine screw and bolt
- Desired greens and embellishments
- Pattern Sheet
- Miscellaneous items: tracing paper, pencil, masking tape, ruler, phillips screwdriver, craft knife, craft scissors, soft cloth, cardboard or cutting mat

1 **Pattern:** Trace pattern onto tracing paper; cut out, leaving ½" (1.3 cm) margin all around. Tape tracing paper pattern backward to a window, and trace reversed pattern to tracing paper. Tape copper sheet to a flat work surface; place cardboard or cutting mat underneath. See Step 2 illustration to measure halfway on the 12" (30.5 cm) edges; mark and draw a line with pen and ruler. Tape patterns on copper along pen line.

2 Transferring: Use transfer paper, or trace by cutting through pattern with a craft knife as shown in the Step 2 illustration. Do not trace cutting line, only design lines. Remove pattern and trace over lines with craft knife or marker; make lines deep enough to show completely on the back side. Place copper sheet facedown, and outline image on the back with the craft knife and marker.

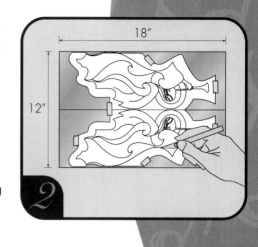

3 Outline: Begin at the top of the angel with the wing, and work down through the halo, face, trumpet and dress. Outline the design area from the back with unsharpened pencil or ballpoint pen, making lines thicker and crisper. Retrace the outline, pushing the area out. Accentuate the outline by tracing again on the front side.

4 Embossing: Push out areas of the copper sheet to give a three-dimesional look. Use an unsharpened pencil, and pressing firmly from the back, see the Step 4 illustration to pretend to color in the desired area while lifting the copper sheet. After embossing, repeat Step 3 to keep outlines clear. Continue to work the copper on both front and back until you are satisfied with the design; keep designs similar on both sides.

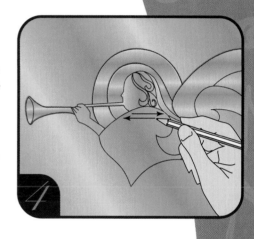

5 Stippling and Cross-hatching: Refer to the pattern for areas. Use the screwdriver to stipple on the back side; tap out dots, some heavy and some light, as on the sleeve, dress and halo. Use the steel-tipped marker on the front side to crosshatch, almost scratching vertical and horizontal lines on the surface. Repeat Step 3 and Step 4, if necessary.

6 Finishing: Place patterns on angels, and trace or transfer cutting line. Repeat Step 1 to mark foldline on back side of copper, and score using a craft knife and ruler. Bend copper carefully along foldline, right side out, making a soft, rounded fold, not a hard crease, or the copper might crack. Use scissors, and cut along marked cutting line, beginning at the bottom of the angel and working up to the fold. Use a soft cloth to rub India ink or shoe polish along lines and textured area. Rub and wipe excess until satisfied with shading.

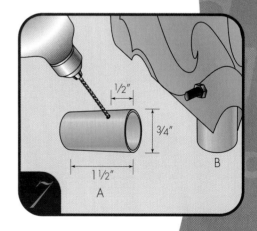

7 Topper Pipe: Drill 2 holes using ¹¹/₆₄" bit ½" (1.3 cm) from 1 end of pipe, as shown in the Step 7A illustration. Use pattern to mark and drill holes on both sides of angel. Wire greens and embellishments together; place inside angel. See 7B to attach copper pipe to angel with machine screw and bolt. Paint screw and bolt copper, or wire or hot-glue greens to hide. Rotate pipe up out of sight for storage or when using angel as a centerpiece.

GILDED
Treetop Star

Stitch this elegant star to top your Christmas tree. The double straight cross-stitch, a simple but bold and striking stitch that resembles a star, is done here in gold metallic yarn. Add pearls and gold beads to create a star that will provide the symbolism of the Star of Bethlehem.

MATERIALS

- 7-mesh plastic canvas, 1½ sheets
- Tapestry needles: Nos. 16, 20, 24
- Yarn: 42 yd. (38.6 m) ivory worsted-weight, 15 yd. (13.8 m) gold metallic plastic canvas
- 7 yd. (6.4 m) lightweight metallic gold thread
- 3 yd. (2.75 m) ivory embroidery floss
- 5 mm pearl pebble beads, 36
- 3 mm gold beads, 144
- Scissors

1 Preparation: See the Plastic Canvas Instructions and Stitches on page 158. Cut two 65x55-bar pieces of canvas and see Stitch Chart to cut, following the bold outlines. Cut up to but not through outer bars.

2 Stitching: See the Stitch Chart to stitch 1 side of each star. Use the No. 16 needle and ivory yarn to work a combination of Gobelin and continental stitches. Fill in all unmarked areas between Gobelin stitches with continental stitches. Use gold plastic canvas yarn to work the double-straight cross-stitches on top of the base stitching.

3 Beads: Cut 1-yd. (0.95 m) lengths of ivory floss and lightweight gold thread. Knot thread ends and weave into back of stitching to secure thread. See the Stitch Chart to position beads in rows between the double crosses. Use No. 20 needle and 1 strand of ivory floss to attach pearl beads with beaded half cross-stitches. Come up at lower left hole, slip bead onto needle and insert needle back through at upper right; each bead will cover 1 continental stitch. Use gold thread and No. 24 needle to attach each gold bead.

4 Finishing: Overcast center bottom opening edges of each star where marked on the Stitch Chart between arrows with gold yarn. Place stars wrong sides together and overcast remaining edges together with gold yarn, leaving bottom opening for placing star over treetop.

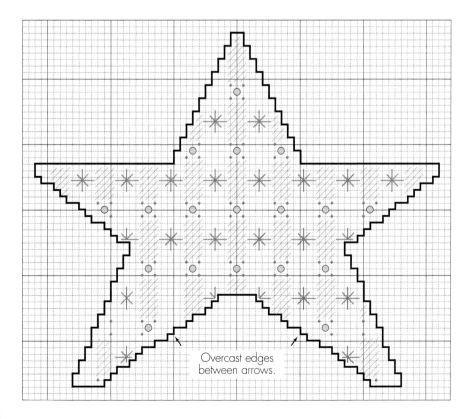

Overcast edges between arrows.

Color Key
/ Ivory Gobelin
✳ Metallic Gold Double Straight Cross
◯ Pearl Bead
• Gold Bead

AROUND *the* HOUSE

All of the decorations that adorn our homes during the Christmas season play a big part in the holiday festivities. Here are some new ideas to spruce up your rooms. From a Poinsettia Print Tablecloth for your dining room to a Mantel Pendulum Clock for your living room fireplace, these crafts will find a cherished place in your home year after year.

Nordic
TABLE RUNNER

Reindeer prance across a line of decorated
Christmas evergreens while snowflakes of
every size float through the air. If you wish
hard enough, you can almost believe these
are the deer that will fly up to the sky
pulling the loaded sleigh and jolly elf
behind them. All these delightful designs
in Scandinavian-inspired colors are
cut from WoolFelt® and embroidered
onto a black background with a variety
of easy stitches in embroidery floss.

MATERIALS

- WoolFelt, 72" (183 cm) wide*: ¾ yd.
  (0.7 m) black for table runner, ¼ yd.
  (0.25 m) each green and red, ⅛ yd.
  (0.15 m) each white, blue and gold
- 1 skein each 6-strand embroidery floss to
  match felt: red, white, gold, blue
- Small sharp scissors
- Pattern Sheet
- Miscellaneous items: tracing paper, pencil,
  scissors, rotary cutter and mat (optional),
  ruler, measuring tape, sewing needle
- *(See Sources on page 159 for purchasing
  information.)

1 Cutting: Trace 4 patterns to tracing paper and cut from felt with small sharp scissors as directed on pattern pieces. To make the cutting of the intricate pieces easier, cut rough outlines around the shapes first, as shown in the Step 1 illustration. Cut a 26" x 60" (66 x 152.5 cm) rectangle for table runner base. Cut 2 each 3½" x 26½" (9 x 67.3 cm) bands from red, green and blue. Cut four ½" x 26½" (1.3 x 67.3 cm) bands from gold. Using a rotary cutter to cut the bands and table runner base will ensure straight clean edges.

2 Embroidering: Use 2 strands of embroidery floss for all embroidery stitches. Refer to page 155 for Embroidery Stitches. You may choose to machine-stitch the shapes and bands, instead of embroidering them by hand. It is not necessary to finish the edges on any of the shapes, bands or the table runner, because WoolFelt does not ravel.

3 Snowflakes: Use 7 large snowflakes on each red band. The remaining snowflakes will be used in the center of the runner. Measure and pin 1 large snowflake in the center of each red band. Pin 3 more on each side of center snowflake, placing them with points in different directions. Use white embroidery floss to stitch the snowflakes to the red bands with a single Smyrna cross in the center.

4 Reindeer: Repeat Step 3 to pin 7 red reindeer on each green band. Use red embroidery floss to stitch the reindeer to green bands with 3 cross-stitches on the body; refer to pattern. Use an eyelet stitch to make the eye, pulling the stitches gently to make a small hole so the green felt shows through the red reindeer and looks like a dark eye. Be careful not to pull too tight and ruin the reindeer; a little bit on each stitch around should do the trick.

5 Trees: Use 8 trees on each blue band. Begin pinning them 1" (2.5 cm) in from each end, and space them evenly across, approximately 1" (2.5 cm) apart. Refer to the Step 5 illustration to stitch the trees to the blue band with 8 Smyrna cross-stitches, randomly placed to look like Christmas tree ornaments: 1 blue, 2 or 3 red, 3 gold and 1 or 2 white.

6 Bands: See the Step 6 illustration to measure and place the bands on each end of the runner. Begin 1" (2.5 cm) from each runner end, and pin the red band. Leave a 2½" (6.5 cm) space, and pin the green band. Measure another 2½" (6.5 cm) space, and pin the blue band. Evenly space the yellow bands between the blue, green and red bands; pin in place.

7 Embroidering Bands: Make a row of backstitches down the center of each gold band with gold floss. Use matching floss to make a row of backstitches 3/16" (4.5 mm) in along each edge of red, green and blue bands. Be careful not to stitch down the reindeer antlers or evergreen tops and trunks.

8 Center Snowflakes: Refer to the photo to scatter and pin the remaining 8 large snowflakes and 14 small snowflakes in the center area of the table runner. Use white embroidery floss to stitch each snowflake to the black table runner with a single Smyrna cross in the center.

CLAY POT
Christmas Tree

Clay pots are coming out of the garden and into the house for the holidays to start a new tree-trimming tradition. Simply paint a trio of clay pots, then stack them to shape the tree. Finish with a generous sprinkling of buttons and bows, and you'll have a new favorite "evergreen" to display year after year!

MATERIALS

- Clay pots: 3½" (9 cm), 4½" (11.5 cm), 6" (15 cm), one each
- 7½" (19.3 cm) clay pot saucer
- Acrylic paints: ivory, light green, dark green, red
- Painting tools: sponge brush, 1½" (3.8 cm) square kitchen sponge
- Gloss varnish
- 40-45 assorted buttons
- Fabric: ⅛" yd. (0.15 m) red plaid, two 4" (10 cm) squares yellow
- 4" (10 cm) square fusible adhesive
- Yellow chenille stem
- Glues: thick white craft, hot glue gun
- Miscellaneous items: tracing paper, pencil, ruler, scissors, pinking shears, craft stick, disposable palette, iron

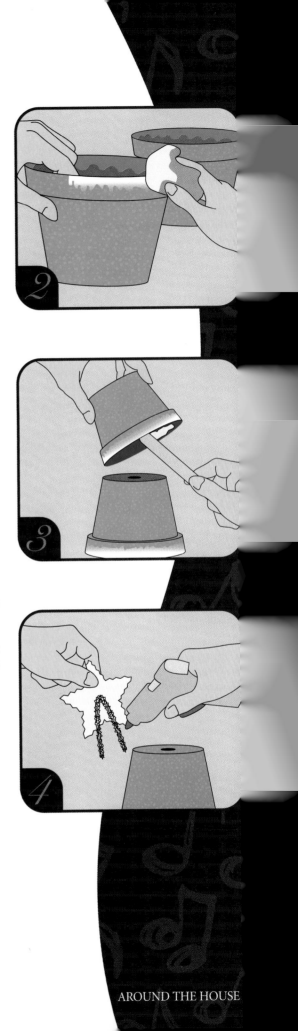

1 Painting: Use the sponge brush to basecoat each clay pot dark green on the outside, and up over the rim to the inside about 1" (2.5 cm). Paint the bottom of the 3½" (9 cm) pot. Paint the clay pot saucer red; let dry.

2 Sponging: Refer to the photo and use the 1½" (3.8 cm) square kitchen sponge to lightly sponge light green onto each pot. Let dry, then sponge ivory onto each pot rim as shown in the Step 2 illustration and photo. Let dry. Apply gloss varnish to each painted pot; let dry.

3 Assembly: See the Step 3 illustration to use the craft stick to liberally apply thick white craft glue to the inner rim edge of the clay pots. Position the saucer upside down on the work surface, and glue the 6" (15 cm) clay pot upside down centered on top of the saucer. Repeat to glue the 4½" (11.5 cm) pot to the 6" (15 cm) pot, then the 3½" (9 cm) pot to the 4½" (11.5 cm) pot. Let dry thoroughly.

4 Star: Refer to the manufacturer's instructions to fuse the yellow fabric squares with wrong sides together. Trace the star pattern to tracing paper, then to yellow fabric. Use pinking shears to cut the star from the fused fabric. Cut an 8" (20.5 cm) piece from the yellow chenille stem for the star holder. Bend the stem in half, then bend the doubled stem in half again. Hot-glue 1 end of the holder to the star. Insert and hot-glue the other end into the clay pot hole in the top of the tree; see the Step 4 illustration.

5 Decorations: Randomly hot-glue buttons to all sides. Also glue a button to the center of the star. Use pinking shears to cut twelve 1" x 4" (2.5 x 10 cm) red plaid fabric strips for the bows. Tie a knot in the center of each strip. Hot-glue a bow to the bottom front and back of the star covering the chenille stem holder; glue remaining bows randomly to the tree.

Star
Cut 1 from fused yellow fabric with pinking shears
1 of 1

Flower & FRUIT VASE

When you need a special table centerpiece at your next holiday gathering, yet you can't spend a small fortune, this stunning bouquet is the answer. Such an arrangement makes a statement, yet doesn't overwhelm your table. The color comes from the fresh fruit and ribbons; the elegance comes from the stark simplicity of three elements— vase, fruit and flowers.

MATERIALS

- Glass vase, 12" to 15" (30.5 to 38 cm) tall, 9" to 10" (23 to 25.5 cm) diameter
- 16-24 green Granny Smith Apples
- 6-9 long white calla lilies (see Flowers)
- 2 yd. (1.85 m) sheer red ribbon
- Miscellaneous items: kitchen sink, sharp knife, scissors, ruler

1 Flowers: Fresh calla lilies and orchids are available from your local florist; either one will work for this arrangement. There are many kinds of orchids from which to choose; white dendrobiums are 1 suggestion. Both callas and orchids should last for at least 3 days in a normal-temperature home; calla lilies are shown in this photo.

2 Preparation: Wash the vase with warm water; let dry. Use glass cleaner or vinegar and water to clean the vase again; let dry thoroughly. If there has been any recent usage with moldy or dirty water in the vase, let it soak overnight in a mild bleach solution.

3 Fruit: Wash and sort through the green apples. Remove any stickers; sort out any apples with nicks or minor imperfections from the perfect apples. If any of the apples appear to have soft or rotten spots, do not use them; they will quickly spoil the water.

4 Filling Vase: Fill the vase half full with green apples. Use the apples with minor imperfections, placing them so the marks face inward and are hidden by other apples. Put water in the vase until it comes to the top of the apples.

5 Lilies: Cut off the bottom 1/2" to 1" (1.3 to 2.5 cm) of the lily stems with a sharp knife, to allow the lilies to begin drawing water up their stems again. See the Step 5 illustration. Cut the lilies to different lengths with the sharp knife as you begin arranging in Step 6, so you can vary their heights in the arrangement.

6 Arranging: See the Step 6 illustration to begin arranging the lilies by placing them in the vase with the stems going into the spaces created by the apples. Refer to the photo to place them in the vase, with heights varying. Continue adding the lilies until all are in the vase. Add more apples and water to securely hold the lilies in place, stopping 1" to 2" (2.5 to 5 cm) from the top of the vase.

7 Caring: Refer to the photo and the Step 7 illustration to tie 2 yd. (1.85 m) of the red ribbon around the neck of the vase. Add water daily, if necessary; it is important to keep the water level to within 1" to 2" (2.5 to 5 cm) of the top of the vase. If the water becomes cloudy or discolored, change it by scooping out as much as you can with a ladle or cup. Then place the vase under a faucet and let the water run until the old water has been displaced. You can also try to pour the old water out, but you might have to redo the arrangement. If only a few lilies begin to wilt, remove those few and rearrange the rest.

ADDITIONAL IDEA

Cranberry Arrangement
Repeat Step 2, using a smaller vase, 8" (20.5 cm) tall. Wash and drain 3-4 bags of cranberries thoroughly, 1 bag at a time. Discard any cranberries that are brown or at all soft. Repeat Steps 4-7 and arrange the orchids using fresh cranberries to hold them in place in the vase. Because cranberries bruise easily, you will need to ease the orchid stems gently down into the fruit.

STARRY
Battenberg Placemat

Although the table linens are not supposed to be the star of any party, these block-printed placemats are sure to be a hit and are very easy to make. Start with a wooden cutout and craft foam to create your own star stamp, and apply black fabric and gold glitter paints. Use a magic marker to make the stars look as if they had been stitched on with metallic gold thread, then finish off by spray painting the lace for a delicate, gleaming border.

1 Star Stamp: Place wooden star on top of craft foam; outline star with a pencil onto foam. Cut out, and glue foam star onto wooden star with tacky glue. Make sure to apply glue evenly all over. Refer to the Step 1 illustration to glue spool to the center of the wooden star for a handle; let dry. Other items that might work for a handle are a small chunk of wood, sachet tablet, pill bottle cap, etc.

2 Preparation: Hand wash placemats; lay flat to dry. Do not use any fabric softeners. Lay placemats on a slightly padded surface, using layers of newspapers or an old folded tablecoth. Mask off the lace border by taping pieces of paper with masking tape strips to cover it up; refer to the Step 3 illustration.

3 Painting: Use the paintbrush to mix the black fabric paint with the glitter fabric paint, about 2/3 black to 1/3 glitter. Use a flat mixing surface such as tinfoil or old foam tray. Apply paint to the foam side of star stamp with brush; use a fairly thick application. Practice stamping on a scrap of fabric first. Place stamp directly onto fabric, do not roll it. Hold the stamp down with 1 hand, and use the other to press gently on each star point for an even paint application; see the Step 3 illustration.

4 Stamped Design: Reapply paint for each star. Fill up the placemat, spacing stars as desired. It is okay to have a partial star stamp along the placemat edges. Simply position stamp so part is on the placemat and the rest is on the paper covering the lace border. Gently remove the tape and paper covering the lace border. When done, let paint dry following manufacturer's instructions.

5 Star Stitching: Use the gold metallic marker to make stitching lines all around the stars, as shown in the Step 5 illustration. Outline the stars first, about 1/4" (6 mm) around each star. Then connect the outlines to the stars with short spokes, spacing them 1/8" to 1/4" (3 to 6 mm) apart. Follow manufacturer's instructions as to usage; if marker has a strong odor, use outside or in a well-ventilated area.

6 Lace Border: Refer to Step 2 to mask off the stamped inner portion of the placemat with paper and masking tape. Use short pieces of tape for curved lines. Make sure that only the Battenberg lace border is exposed. Place the placemat on several layers of newspaper. Work outside or in a well-ventilated area. Follow manufacturer's instructions to spray the lace with gold spray paint. Spray evenly using a sweeping motion. Repeat, if needed for complete coverage.

7 Care and Laundering: Follow manufacturer's instructions to heat-set fabric paint. Hand wash, lay flat to dry, and iron only on the reverse side.

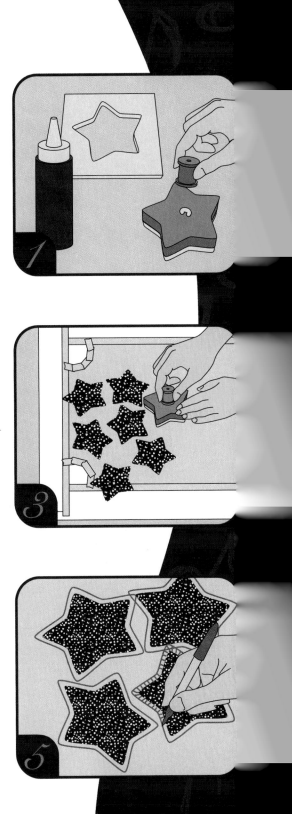

Birdhouse
CHRISTMAS VILLAGE

This Christmas village of painted birdhouses is as handsome as any collectible village found in stores, but much more valuable because it is made by you. Display it year-round but add fresh greens for a seasonal look!

MATERIALS

- Wood birdhouses*: 4.25" x 4.625" x 5" (10.8 x 11.8 x 12.5 cm) stoves and tinware; 4.5" x 5.25" x 5.25" (11.5 x 13.2 x 13.2 cm) livery; 4" x 4.25" x 9" (10 x 10.8 x 23 cm) hotel; 5.75" x 5" x 4.5" (14.5 x 12.5 x 11.5 cm) bank; 4.75" x 7" x 4.5" (12 x 18 x 11.5 cm) antiques; 5" x 5" x 4" (12.5 x 12.5 x 10 cm) barber
- Acrylic paints: adobe, tan, light gray, soft black, gold, yellow, red, pine green, green apple, pumpkin, mushroom, terra-cotta, pale teal green, pale blue, gray blue, soldier blue, burnt sienna, white
- Paintbrushes: No. 6, No. 1 fine liner, sponge brush
- Wood sealer
- Wood filler
- Permanent-ink black pen
- 1/4" (6 mm) dowel, 3" (7.5 cm)
- White craft glue
- Clear acrylic spray
- Water-base varnish (optional)
- Pattern Sheet
- Miscellaneous items: tracing and graphite paper, pencil, stylus, fine sandpaper, tack cloth, disposable palette, water container, paper towels, masking tape
- * (See Sources on page 159 for purchasing information.)

1 Preparation: See page 156 for Painting Instructions and Techniques. Sand each birdhouse and wipe with tack cloth. Fill nail holes with wood filler; let dry. Sand to remove excess; wipe with tack cloth. Use the sponge brush to apply wood sealer to each house. Let dry; sand lightly. Refer to the Paint Color Chart on page 103 and use the sponge brush to basecoat each building and roof. If needed, apply 2 coats; let dry between coats.

2 Patterns: Trace the patterns onto tracing paper. Position and tape each traced pattern on appropriate birdhouse. Slide graphite paper under tracing paper and use the stylus to trace pattern lines. Do not trace the barber pole, it is only for placement, or the greenery lines, they will be added later. It is not necessary to transfer the curtain folds, window and shutter lines or the livery board lines. They will be drawn in with marker freehand.

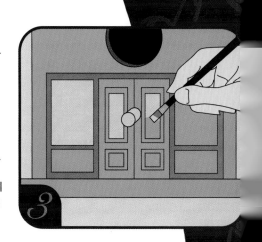

3 Painting Buildings: Refer to the photo and the Paint Color Chart. Paint the details using the No. 6 flat or liner brush. Two colors joined by a + in the Color Chart means to mix the 2 together in equal amounts. Basecoat all "glass" windows with pale blue; see the Step 3 illustration. Paint ¼" (6 mm) red and white stripes on the dowel for the barber pole.

4 Greenery: Paint the greenery (swags, wreaths, trees) freehand, or transfer a single line in the center, such as an oval for a wreath. Use 3 shades of green and work from darkest to lightest: pine green for the dark, pale teal green for the medium and green apple for the light. Refer to the Step 4 illustration to use the liner brush and make short spiky lines outward from center of the greenery, to look like pine needles. Paint the ribbons red and the Christmas tree trims red and yellow.

5 Details: Use the black pen to trace all detail lines and make the sign lettering; see Step 5 illustration. For the Stoves and Tinware, outline door and window trim and make lines on window panels. For the Livery, sketch vertical board lines approximately 1/4" (6 mm) apart on the walls, and 1/8" (3 mm) on doors and windows. For the Hotel, outline all bricks, and door, sign and window trim. For the Bank, outline bell, lights and door trim. For the Antiques, outline door, window and sign trims, and antiques in window. For the Barber, refer to the photo to glue striped pole on front, and draw door handle and light lines.

6 Roofs: Use the black pen to draw all lines. Stoves and Tinware Roof: Make black horizontal lines 1/4" to 3/8" (6 mm to 1 cm) apart on each roof side. Livery Roof: Mix a small amount of terra-cotta and burnt sienna to dry-brush the roof. Wipe brush and use a light touch to pull long strokes with flat edge of brush to suggest rust on a tin roof. Let dry. Draw three vertical black lines 1 1/4" (3.2 cm) apart on each roof section. Bank and Barber Roofs: Draw lines for square and curved shingles on each roof side.

7 Finishing: Lightly spray several coats of acrylic spray on each building. If heavier finish is desired, apply several coats of varnish.

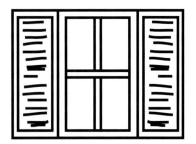

Stoves and Tinware Side Window

Barber Side Window

Barber Side Window

Birdhouse Christmas Village

Windows & Corner Trim

Trace 1 of each window, or set of windows for hotel, centered on appropriate building side.

Trace Hotel brick corner trim 2 times on each corner. Refer to photo for placement.

7 of 7

Livery Side Window

Hotel Brick Corner Trim

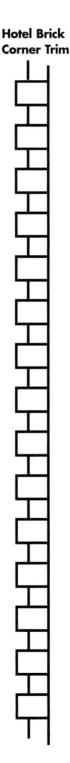

Hotel Side Window
Space ¾" apart

PAINT COLOR CHART

STOVES AND TINWARE

Basecoat	Pale Teal Green
Roof	Terra-Cotta
Window Frames	Pumpkin
Door/Window Trim and Sign	Adobe

LIVERY

Basecoat	Terra-Cotta
Roof	Light Gray
Door/Window Trim and Sign	Tan

HOTEL

Basecoat	Pumpkin
Roof	Soft Black
Center Brick of Arch Window Trim	Terra-Cotta
Bricks and Sign/Window/Door Trim	Tan
Door/Sign	White

BANK

Basecoat	Light Gray
Roof	Pumpkin
Doors	Tan
Door Trim/Lights	Light Gray + Soft Black
Bell	Gold
Light Bulbs	Yellow

ANTIQUES

Basecoat	Mushroom
Roof	Pine Green
Window/Door/Sign Trim	Terra-Cotta
Sign/Curtains	Adobe
Door	Soft Black
Basket	Burnt Sienna + Tan
Decoy	Burnt Sienna
Lamp	Soldier Blue
Jug	Mushroom + White

BARBER

Basecoat	Gray Blue
Roof	Soldier Blue
Door/Signs	White/Soft Black Outline
Door Panel/Light	Soft Black
Light Bulb	Yellow
Side Window Trim	Soldier Blue

Snowman
DOOR DOLLY

With his extra-long button arms, this snowman will hang around your house for many years. He will be a cheerful greeter for guests and family alike, and construction with foam balls and paper twist make him a breeze to create.

MATERIALS

- 2 pieces 18" x 24" (46 x 61 cm) white tissue paper
- 1 yd. (0.95 m) each paper twist: red, black
- Styrofoam® balls: 4" (10 cm), 5" (12.5 cm)
- Flat buttons: eight ¼" (6 mm) black; two ⅜" (1 cm) black; approximately 100 assorted ½" to 1" (1.3 to 2.5 cm) white
- Wood: six ¾" (2 cm) spools; two 1¼" (3.2 cm) knobs with hole; two 1" (2.5 cm) beads
- Acrylic paints: white, black, red
- ½ yd. (0.5 m) plaid Christmas ribbon, 1¼" (3.2 cm) wide
- 3 white chenille stems
- 1" (2.5 cm) wood or plastic carrot
- Mini holly sprig
- Craft wire: 18" (46 cm) of 24-gauge, 3" (7.5 cm) of 18-gauge
- Glues: glue stick, white craft; low-temp glue gun
- Miscellaneous items: serrated knife, scissors, ruler, wire cutters, small paintbrush

1 Body: Use serrated knife to slice 1" (2.5 cm) from back of 5" (12.5 cm) ball. Fold 1 piece of tissue paper to 12" x 18" (30.5 x 46 cm). Use glue stick to glue both 12" (30.5 cm) edges together. Lay body ball, flat edge down, in center of tissue paper. Wrap tissue paper into a tube around ball, bringing glued edges together. Mark tissue paper where the seam should be, leaving tube a little loose; use glue stick to glue together. Gather and wire with 4" (10 cm) of 24-gauge wire ½" (1.3 cm) from 1 end. Use paintbrush handle to make a hole ½" (1.3 cm) deep and wide in top and bottom of body ball. Hot-glue gathered end of tissue in hole as shown in the Step 1 illustration. Gently invert tissue tube and ease tissue up and around body; gather other end and hot-glue into opposite hole.

2 Head: Fold tissue paper to 9" x 24" (23 x 61 cm), cut off 1 end to 9" x 14" (23 x 35.5 cm). Repeat second half of Step 1 to glue tissue into a tube, and wire and hot-glue to cover 4" (10 cm) ball. Insert 18-gauge wire in hole to join head and body. **Do not glue.**

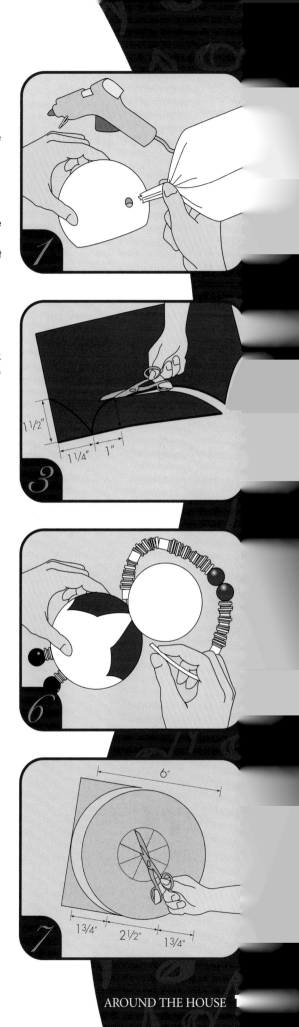

3 Vest: Cut four 4½" (11.5 cm) lengths of red paper twist and use craft glue to glue together on 4½" (11.5 cm) sides. Fold in half widthwise and see the Step 3 illustration to cut. Gather top edge to fit around body; glue. Refer to the photo to glue three ¼" (6 mm) black buttons to vest.

4 Legs: Paint 1¼" (3.2 cm) knobs black for feet. Let dry. Cut two 1½" (3.8 cm) pieces from chenille stem. Insert and hot-glue 1 end into black knob foot. Thread 5 white buttons on chenille stem and hot-glue stems into bottom of body.

5 Arms: Paint 1" (2.5 cm) beads red for hands and wood spools white. Let dry. Wire and hot-glue 2 remaining chenille stems together overlapping 1" (2.5 cm). On 1 end, thread on 2 red beads, 2" (5 cm) of white buttons, spool, 1¼" (3.2 cm) of white buttons, spool, 2½" (6.5 cm) of white buttons, and spool. Use opposite end of chenille stem and repeat to thread on other arm.

6 Assembly: See the Step 6 illustration to center arms on chenille stem and wrap ends around neck; hot-glue. Hot-glue head to body. Tie plaid ribbon into a bow and hot-glue to neck. Hot-glue two ⅜" (1 cm) black button eyes and five ¼" (6 mm) black buttons for mouth. Glue on carrot nose.

7 Hat Brim: Cut and untwist two 12" (30.5 cm) lengths of black paper twist. Glue together on 12" (30.5 cm) sides. Fold in half and glue to make a 6" (15 cm) square. See the Step 7 illustration to cut a 6" (15 cm) circle for hat brim. Draw a 2½" (6.5 cm) circle in the center, and cut 8 slits in the center circle.

8 Hat Crown: Cut and untwist two 3" (7.5 cm) lengths of black paper twist; glue together on 3" (7.5 cm) sides. Fold 1 end 1" (2.5 cm) toward center for top of hat. Cut and untwist a 3" (7.5 cm) length of black paper twist. Cut a 2½" (6.5 cm) circle and glue to top of hat. Glue wedges on hat brim to inside of hat crown. Cut a 10" (25.5 cm) length of red paper twist and glue around hat crown. Glue mini holly sprig to 1 side of hat crown with stem tucked behind red twist.

Snowflake VASE

No potter's wheel is necessary for the sleek lines of this contemporary vase. Instead, use a rolling pin to make a sheet of clay that, formed over a foam cone, becomes the vase. Decorate it with clay snowflake cutouts, wash with white paint, and you have added sophistication to your holiday decor.

MATERIALS

- 5-lb. (2.2 kg) box Mexican Pottery Clay*
- 24" x 18" (61 x 46 cm) rolling cloth
- Various-size plastic or lace doilies
- 15" x 4" (38 x 10 cm) Styrofoam® cone
- Brushes: small watercolor, 1" (2.5 cm) sponge
- 2 small plastic canvas shapes: circle, octagon
- White acrylic paint
- Gold acrylic spray paint
- Water-based polyurethane
- 12" (30.5 cm) three-legged stand
- Miscellaneous items: masking tape, steak knife, rolling pin, small sponges, water container, ruler, pencil, spatula, plastic wrap, fork, fan, tracing paper, table knife, paint palette, soft rags
- *(See Sources on page 159 for purchasing information.)

1 Rolling: Place rolling cloth on smooth work surface; secure with masking tape. Cut clay block into ½" (1.3 cm) thick slices with steak knife. Lay slices flat on cloth, overlapping slightly, to form a large rectangle. Use rolling pin to smooth clay, making a large flat sheet ¼" (6 mm) thick. Use damp sponge and water to fix any cracks; clay is water soluble, and too much water will make it break down.

2 Cutting: See the Assembly Guide to measure and lightly trace vase on the clay sheet with a pencil. Cut out with a steak knife; do not mark any of the details. Loosen vase from cloth with spatula or by lifting cloth; place back on cloth. Lay doilies on clay randomly and at differing angles; press gently into clay with damp sponge and trace along outer edges with pencil. Loosen vase from cloth again; lay back on cloth.

3 Molding: Leave plastic on foam cone to prevent clay from sticking; if there is none, wrap in plastic wrap. Mark a line 2″ (5 cm) up from wide end of foam cone. Place cone on clay, with the bottom edge at the line; see the Step 3 illustration. Roll the clay onto the cone loosely, so it may be removed easily. Refer to the photo to see how vase overlaps at the bottom, but is open at the top.

4 Seam: Make a slip of 2 tbsp. (25 mL) each clay and water; mix to a ketchuplike consistency. Use fork to gently score the overlapping edges with crosshatch lines ½″ (1.3 cm) in. Apply slip liberally to scored surface with watercolor brush. Press edges together, applying light pressure with fingers until clay holds. Take a small ball of clay, and make 3 clay worms, about 5″ (12.5 cm) long. Work the worms into the seam with fingers; smooth with sponge and water. Cut a circle to fit the vase bottom; score and slip before applying. Place vase on its side in front of fan for 1 hour, seam first, rotating ⅓ every 20 minutes. Ease cone out, then place vase upside down on cone to apply the snowflakes.

5 Diamond Snowflakes: Cut 3 diamond shapes from clay with steak knife, 1″ (2.5 cm), ¾″ (2 cm), and ½″ (1.3 cm) in width. Roll 3 small balls of clay and press flat onto diamonds for snowflake centers. Texture them with a plastic canvas shape. Refer to photo and Assembly Guide for placement along seam.

6 Applying Snowflakes: Follow Step 4 to score the vase and snowflake backs, brush on slip, and apply snowflakes to vase. Make 16 small balls of clay, and use 4 or 6 on each snowflake for points; refer to Assembly Guide and photo. Apply with slip, and work with fingers to elongate balls into points and into vase surface. Make 4 holes in middle snowflake with end of paintbrush.

7 Octagon Snowflakes: Cut 4 squares from clay with steak knife, 1½″ (3.8 cm) in width. See the Step 7A illustration to place 1 square over the other; cut off points to make an octagon. Repeat Steps 5 and 6 to make snowflake centers, and apply as shown in Assembly Guide. Make 8 small balls of clay, using 4 on each snowflake for points. Press serrated steak knife blade on its side at corners for design; see 7B.

8 Finishing: Add additional small clay shapes as desired or as shown in Assembly Guide. Smooth any rough areas with sponge and water. Set vase in stand to harden for 5 to 6 days. Spray-paint stand gold; let dry. Place vase in stand. Mix 1 tbsp. (15 mL) white paint with a few drops of water; use sponge brush to paint. Add more water if you want it more transparent, more paint if you want it whiter. This first coat will seal clay; work quickly because clay is water soluble. Let dry for at least 1 hour; apply additional coats as desired. Apply polyurethane with sponge brush; let dry following manufacturer's instructions. Spray gold paint onto soft rag, and wipe over snowflakes.

Assembly Guide

Gift Box
POT HOLDERS

These pot holders are machine-quilted, making them great projects for both experienced and novice quilters. The clever gift box design done with quilting, ribbon and contrasting fabric couldn't be easier. Enlarge the pattern on a photocopy machine, and you can create festive placemats to grace your holiday table.

MATERIALS

For Each Pot Holder
- Cotton fabrics, ¼ yd. (0.25 m) each: solid red for backing; red/gold print, red/green/gold stripe or holly stripe
- ¼ yd. (0.25 m) fusible fleece
- 1 yd. (0.95 m) metallic gold ribbon, ⅛" (3 mm) wide, for red/gold pot holder
- Pattern Sheet
- Miscellaneous items: tracing paper, pencil, scissors, iron, ruler, straight pins, sewing machine, matching threads, sewing needle, air-soluble pen or chalk pencil

1 Preparation: Trace the pattern onto tracing paper and cut out from desired fabrics as indicated on the pattern. Mark quilting lines on pot holder front with air-soluble pen or chalk pencil. Omit seam allowance when cutting fleece. Fuse fleece to wrong side of backing fabric.

2 Red/Gold Pot Holder: Baste gold ribbon to right side of front fabric, following markings on pattern. Cut 5″ (12.5 cm) of ribbon and fold in half for hanger. Pin hanger to right side of front fabric at top corner, with loop toward center and ends outward; see the Step 2 illustration. Baste the hanger ⅛″ (3 mm) from edge of fabric.

3 Striped & Holly Pot Holders: Stitch box lid appliqué pieces along center seam, right sides together. Press seam allowance under and pin to pot holder front along the quilting lines; see the Step 3 illustration. Machine-baste the box lid pieces ¼″ (6 mm) in from edges.

4 Hanger: Cut a 1½″ x 5″ (3.8 x 12.5 cm) red/green/gold fabric strip for the striped pot holder and a 1½″ x 18″ (3.8 x 46 cm) red fabric strip for the holly pot holder. Fold in half lengthwise, and then again; stitch along open edge. Cut 5″ (12.5 cm) from red strip. See instructions and illustration in Step 2 to baste 5″ (12.5 cm) strips to pot holders for hangers.

5 Pot Holder Assembly: Stitch pot holder back and front right sides together with hanger sandwiched in between. Leave a 3″ (7.5 cm) opening for turning. Turn right side out; slipstitch opening closed. Press.

6 Quilting: Stitch along the box lid edges, and marked front center quilting line; see the Step 6 illustration. Also quilt along center of gold ribbon on red/gold pot holder. Remove basting threads on box lid pieces.

7 Finishing: Make a 4″ (10 cm) bow from gold ribbon for red/gold pot holder and from remaining red fabric strip for holly pot holder. Tack to center top.

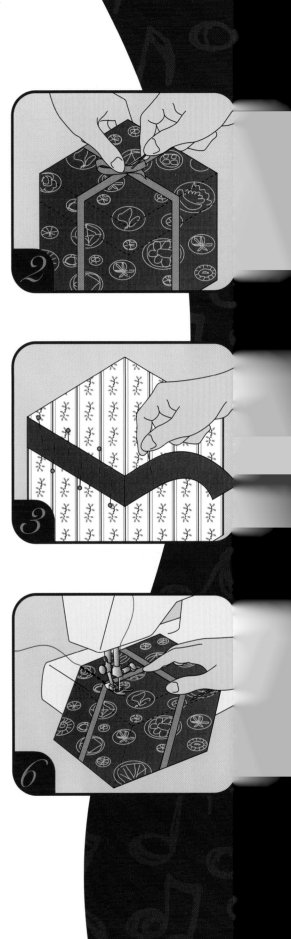

Cup of Tea
CORNER SHELF

This delightful corner shelf in the shape of a Christmas tree is perfect for displaying miniatures. Decorated as shown with wooden teacup cutouts and teapot and teacup rubber stamps, this shelf might remind you to have that special cup of Christmas tea with a loved one whom you haven't seen in a long time. Or you could choose instead to embellish the shelf with designs that match your favorite collectibles.

MATERIALS

- Wooden prestained green Christmas tree corner shelf, 11" x 12.6" x 7" (28 x 32 x 18 cm)*
- 4 wooden cutout miniature teacups, 9/16" x 1" (1.4 x 2.5 cm)*
- Rubber stamps*: teacup, teapot, circle, daisy
- Artist's brush: fine liner, No. 4 flat
- Small black ink pad
- Acrylic craft paints: red, metallic gold
- 4 small gold round-head nails
- Miscellaneous items: fine sandpaper, tack cloth, paint palette, tape measure, pencil, hammer
- *(See Sources on page 159 for purchasing information.)

1 Preparation: Refer to page 156 for Painting Instructions and Techniques. Lightly sand wooden teacup cutouts and shelf, if unfinished; remove dust with tack cloth. If corner shelf is unfinished, basecoat with green paint using a 1" (2.5 cm) sponge brush, or use a soft cloth and stain it green.

2 Stamping: Press rubber stamps firmly and evenly onto the wooden surface. Do not roll stamps; reapply paint or ink after each use. Refer to the photo for placement.

3 Wooden Teacup Cutouts: Use the No. 4 flat brush to basecoat the front and back sides of the wooden teacup cutouts with red paint; do not paint the edges. Let dry; paint the edges metallic gold. See the Step 3 illustration to apply metallic gold paint with the No. 4 flat brush to the flower only of the daisy stamp, and stamp once in the center of each teacup on the front.

4 Edge Design: Apply metallic gold paint with the No. 4 flat brush to the circle stamp, and stamp along the edges of the shelf. Let dry. Use the handle end of the liner brush to make a dot in the center of each circle with red paint. Let dry.

5 Teapot and Teacup Stamps: Apply black ink to teapot stamp, and stamp in the center of the bottom shelf. Apply black ink to teacup stamp, and stamp 2 teacups randomly on each vertical side between the 2 shelves; refer to photo. Apply metallic gold paint with the No. 4 flat brush to the flower only of the daisy stamp, and stamp randomly on the top shelf and around the teapot on the bottom shelf. Let ink dry 6 to 8 hours.

6 Painting Stamps: See the Step 6 illustration to use the liner brush to paint the teapot and teacup backgrounds red, and the stars and trim metallic gold. Let dry.

7 Finishing: Use a tape measure to measure along the edge of the top shelf. Divide into 4 equal parts, and lightly mark with a pencil. See the Step 7 illustraton to hold a teacup handle to the mark, and pound the nail into the shelf edge at the mark, hanging up the teacup at the same time. Nail heads should be large enough to hold on the teacups. Refer to photo to hang the teacups with the handles facing outward.

Nutcrackers *SWEET*

This pillow and doll in a nutcracker design are a delightful duo! Fuse fabric and ribbons on a pillow to make the nutcracker soldier's stately uniform and crown. In no time he'll be standing at attention. The doll is fashioned from painted foam, fabric arms, legs and boots, and sports a wool mustache and hair.

MATERIALS

For Pillow
- 14" (35.5 cm) square white pillow with removable pillow cover* (See instructions on page 158 for making your own pillow cover.)
- Cotton fabrics, 4" (10 cm) square each: royal blue, brown, red pin-dot, black, white, pale pink
- Trims: ⅓ yd. (0.32 m) gold lamé ribbon, 3" (7.5 cm) wide; ¼ yd. (0.25 m) metallic gold woven ribbon, ⅞" (2.2 cm) wide; ⅛ yd. (0.15 m) each: metallic gold baby rickrack and ½" (1.3 cm) gold braid; 1⅔ yd. (1.58 m) red/green stripe grosgrain ribbon, ⅞" (2.2 cm) wide; 1⅓ yd. (1.27 m) each: metallic gold wire-edge ribbon, 1" (2.5 cm) wide and metallic gold rickrack
- ⅓ yd. (0.32 m) fusible web
- 1⅔ yd. (1.58 m) fusible tape, ⅞" (2.2 cm) wide
- Black fine-line fabric marker
- Fabric glue

For Doll
- Styrofoam® balls, 1 each: 1" (2.5 cm); 1½" (3.8 cm); 2¼" (6 cm); 4" (10 cm); 5" (12.5 cm)
- 45" (115 cm) cotton mini-print fabrics: ½ yd. (0.5 m) royal blue, ⅛ yd. (0.15 m) red pin-dot
- Felt: 8" (20.5 cm) square black, 1" x 1½" (2.5 x 3.8 cm) white
- 4" x 16" (10 x 40.5 cm) polyester batting
- Polyester fiberfill
- 3½" x 12" (9 x 30.5 cm) fusible web
- Brown wool doll hair
- Assorted gold trims: 1⅓ yd. (1.27 m) ribbon, ¾" (2 cm) wide; ½ yd. (0.5 m) ribbon, ⅜" (1 cm) wide; 1½ yd. (1.4 m) braid, ½" (1.3 cm) wide; ⅔ yd. (0.63 m) flat braid, ⅞" (2.2 cm) wide; 2 small tassels, or ⅛ yd. (0.15 m) fringe braid
- 2" (5 cm) black pom-pom
- 18 mm wiggle eyes, two
- Round gold beads: 7 mm, 18; 5 mm, four; 4 mm, three
- Paints: pink acrylic spray, black dimensional fabric
- Low-temp glue gun
- Pattern Sheet
- Miscellaneous items: tracing paper, pencil, scissors, ruler, iron, serrated knife, floral pins, T-pins, 3" (7.5 cm) wood pick, sewing machine, matching sewing threads

PILLOW

1 Preparation: Wash and dry pillow cover and fabrics; do not use fabric softener. Trace the patterns onto tracing paper, and cut out.

2 Patterns: Follow manufacturer's instructions to apply fusible web to wrong side of fabric pieces and gold lamé ribbon. Trace the patterns onto paper backing of fused fabrics as marked on patterns, and cut belt, cuffs and crown brim from woven metallic ribbon.

3 Fusing: Remove paper backings and refer to the Step 3 illustration to position the boots. Refer to the illustration and photo to place appliqués onto the pillow cover front. Fuse 1 at a time in the following order: boots, legs, jacket, hair, face, eyes, nose, pupils, beard, teeth, crown, crown top and hands. Do not overlap pieces except for 1/8" (3 mm) of the jacket over the legs and the crown brim over the crown top.

4 Nutcracker Details: Use black fabric marker to draw lines for arms on jacket, teeth, beard and mustache. Cut and glue gold braid to shoulders for epaulets and baby rickrack to boot tops for trim; glue belt, cuff and crown brim.

5 Borders: Apply fusible tape to striped grosgrain ribbon. Fuse ribbon to pillow cover front, 3/4" (2 cm) from edge, mitering corners. Spot-glue mitered corners as needed. Glue gold rickrack 1/2" (1.3 cm) inside ribbon border; miter corners. Refer to photo to fuse snowflakes in pillow corners.

6 Finishing: Cut gold wire-edge ribbon into 12" (30.5 cm) lengths and tie each into a small bow. Tack or glue a bow to each corner of mitered ribbon border. When pillow cover is dry, insert pillow form.

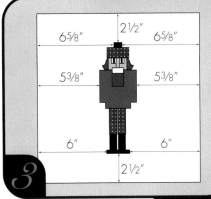

PILLOW

DOLL

1 Body: Use serrated knife to cut a 1/4" (6 mm) slice from each side of 5" (12.5 cm) foam ball. Cut an 18" (46 cm) circle from blue fabric. Fold and mark 4 equal sections along outer edge. Place foam ball in center of fabric circle. Begin at 1 mark and use knife tip to tuck fabric into flat surface at top of ball; see the Step 1 illustration. Repeat for remaining marks and again for fabric between marks.

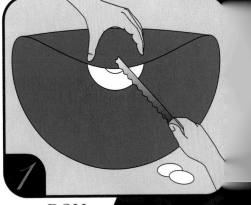

DOLL

2 Arms & Legs: Trace the patterns and cut out. Sew arms and legs right sides together using a ¼" (6 mm) seam allowance; leave tops open. Turn right side out and stuff lightly with fiberfill. Fold under a small hem at top and hot-glue closed. Tuck arms into either side of body at top; spot-glue. Hot-glue legs under body so that feet stick up when sitting; secure with T-pins. Hot-glue toe seam of each boot, slip over foot, and glue back seam.

3 Head: Cut a small slice from one side of 4" (10 cm) foam ball; cut the 1" and 1½" (2.5 and 3.8 cm) balls in half. Spray foam pieces pink; let dry. Hot-glue 1½" (3.8 cm) foam pieces to head for cheeks. Squeeze ½" (1.3 cm) piece to resemble a nose; glue to face. Glue on wiggle eyes.

4 Hair, Mustache & Beard: Cut a ½" x 4" (1.3 x 10 cm) piece of wool hair for mustache; twist and hot-glue under nose. Trim and curl up around cheeks. Cut four 4" (10 cm) lengths of wool for hair. Fold in half and attach 2 pieces with T-pin to either side of face. Cut three 2" (5 cm) pieces of wool for beard. Glue to front of body where chin will be. Use wood pick and glue gun to attach head to body, positioning chin over beard, and as shown in the Step 4 illustration. Refer to the photo to draw teeth on white felt with black paint; let dry. Glue in place between mustache and beard.

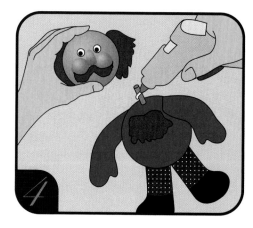

5 Hat: Cut a 3½" x 12" (9 x 30.5 cm) piece of red fabric. Follow manufacturer's instructions to apply fusible web to wrong side of fabric. Cut two 12" (30.5 cm) lengths of ⅞" (2.2 cm) braid and a 12" (30.5 cm) length of ¾" (2 cm) ribbon. Refer to the photo and the Step 5A illustration to decorate 12" (30.5 cm) edge of red fabric. Overlap and hot-glue ends to make a tube. Hot-glue eleven 7 mm beads to ribbon evenly spaced around tube. Cut 2¼" (6 cm) ball in half and insert 1 half inside tube. Fold top edge of fabric down ½" (1.3 cm) and hot-glue to ball half as shown in 5B. Hot-glue pom-pom to top of hat. Place hat on head and hot-glue or pin.

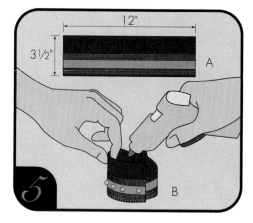

6 Finishing: Refer to the photo to glue ribbon and braid trims. Glue 5 mm beads to cuff trim for buttons, 4 mm beads to belt and 7 mm beads to body front and front of boots.

Christmas EXPRESS

All aboard the Christmas Express! Little wood blocks and tiny wheels come together in the twinkling of an eye to bring you a trainload of wishes. If your mantel can hold more Christmas cheer, simply purchase bigger blocks and wheels.

1 Painting: Use round paintbrush to paint 7 blocks and the spool with red, and 8 blocks with green. Let dry. Apply another coat of paint. Cut the toothpick to ¾" (2 cm) with the wire cutters. Hot-glue a wheel on each end for an axle. Paint all wheels and toothpick axle with 1 coat of gold paint. For easier painting, hold wheel on tip of pencil. Let dry.

2 Lettering: Refer to the photo and use paint marker to print 1 white letter on each block, leaving ¼" (6 mm) border at bottom for wheels. On the red blocks, print M, R, Y, H, I, T, and A. On the green blocks, print E, R, C, R, S, M, and S. Let dry. On the remaining green block, draw a white rectangle window for the engine.

3 Assembly: Refer to the Step 3 illustration to hot-glue 4 wheels, 2 per side, to the lower corners of each block. Check to make sure each block stands level. Hot-glue 1 wheel to an end of red spool. Hot-glue other end to front of engine block. Hot-glue toothpick axle under front end of spool. Place the engine block first, then line up all the other blocks in order to spell "Merry Christmas."

MATERIALS

- Wood shapes: fifteen ¾" (2 cm) blocks; ¾" (2 cm) wood spool; sixty-three ½" (1.3 cm) wood wheels
- Acrylic paints: red, green, metallic gold
- No. 5 round paintbrush
- White paint marker
- Hot glue gun
- Miscellaneous items: round toothpick, ruler, wire cutters, pencil

Goldie LAWN ANGEL

One person's trash bag is another person's treasure. Perched on your front porch or in your yard, this angel will bring a chorus of kudos from friends and neighbors, who'll never believe she's made from kitchen trash bags over a foam armature!

MATERIALS

- Styrofoam® shapes*: two 6" x 24" (15 x 61 cm) cones; 1" x 12" x 36" (2.5 x 30.5 x 91.5 cm) sheet; 6" (15 cm) ball; cake dummies, one each: 3" x 10" (7.5 x 25.5 cm) and 3" x 12" (7.5 x 30.5 cm)
- 6 white tall kitchen trash bags with twist ties
- 3 yd. (2.75 m) amber cellophane, 24" (61 cm) wide
- Garlands: 4 yd. (3.7 m) metallic gold star; 5 yd. (4.6 m) metallic gold looped; 1/2 yd. (0.5 m) iridescent tinsel, 2" (5 cm) wide
- 3 yd. (2.75 m) gold foil wire-edge ribbon, 2" (5 cm) wide
- Floral sprays: peach, mauve, ivory, gold metallic
- 5 white chenille stems
- 16" (40.5 cm) wood dowel, 3/8" (1 cm) wide
- Metallic gold glitter
- 18-gauge floral wire
- Floral pins
- Low-temp glue gun
- Miscellaneous items: serrated knife, scissors, wire cutters, pliers, 2 wire hangers, 5-lb. (2.2 kg) coffee can, knitting needle, tape measure, newspaper, saw
- * (See Sources on page 159 for purchasing information.)

1 Preparation: Use the serrated knife to cut from the foam sheet: two 1" x 24" (2.5 x 61 cm) strips, 3" x 24" (7.5 x 61 cm) strip, 5-pointed 6" (15 cm) star. Cut the 1" (2.5 cm) strips into the following lengths: four 1" (2.5 cm) and two each 6" (15 cm), 5" (12.5 cm), and 3" (7.5 cm). Cut wood dowel into two 8" (20.5 cm) lengths.

2 Base and Torso: Refer to the Assembly Guide; use low-temp glue gun. Center and glue cake dummies. Insert and glue 5" (12.5 cm) of wood dowel through the center of the discs. Glue the four 1" (2.5 cm) foam squares around the wood dowel for support. Shape the top end of the 3" (7.5 cm) foam strip to cradle the ball head. Insert and glue 4" (10 cm) of the remaining wood dowel for the neck. Press the opposite end onto the dowel extending from the base; glue. Attach the 24" (61 cm) cones to the torso sides with glue and floral pins.

3 Dress: Turn 4 trash bags inside out; double the bags. Place the body, base down, inside a bag; gather and pin the bag tops. Pull the other bag down over the body, poking the neck dowel through. Wrap a chenille stem around the base at neck. Tie wire-edge ribbon around waist; fold streamers in half lengthwise and curl loosely around fingers.

4 Arms: Cut the hook off a wire hanger; straighten wire to 41" (104 cm). Center wire around dowel neck and twist once to make a loop; remove. Use a knitting needle to make a hole lengthwise through the center of 6 foam pieces; slide onto wire as shown in the Step 4 illustration. Bend a small loop at the wire end for hands.

5 Sleeves: Gather the bottom 2" (5 cm) of 2 arm trash bags; twist 6" (15 cm) of wire around. Insert wire through hand loops; twist to secure. Open the trash bags and pull back up over arms to cover foam; see the Step 5 illustration. Slide arm loop over neck and wrap a chenille stem around the bag at each arm top, leaving 2" (5 cm) extending. Refer to the photo to position the arms; tie bag ends around the neck.

6 Head: Insert knitting needle in foam ball for a handle. Lightly spray with peach, all over; with mauve, working from the back toward the cheeks; and with ivory, down the face center and above cheeks to highlight. Wrap the looped garland around the head for hair; secure with floral pins. Glue the head on the dowel neck.

7 Halo: Cut the hook from hanger; straighten the wire. Wrap the wire around a coffee can and twist the ends together, leaving a 5" (12.5 cm) stem. Spray the halo with gold; let dry. Cut 3 yd. (2.75 m) of star garland and wind around the halo. Insert and glue stem into the head.

8 Star: Pin and glue a ½" (1.3 cm) chenille stem loop to an interior point. Spray star with gold and glue glitter on each side; let dry between paint and glitter. Insert 1 end of the star garland through the loop; twist. Loop opposite end around angel's hands.

9 Wings: Fan-fold cellophane widthwise at 1-yd. (0.95 m) intervals. Gather at center and twist floral wire around center of wings; bend ends into a hook. Gently open cellophane into a large bow. Lightly spray wings with gold; let dry. Tie tinsel garland loosely around neck; knot at back. Hook wings over tinsel; pinch hook closed. Use floral pins to secure wings to back. Place bricks inside the angel's skirt for stability.

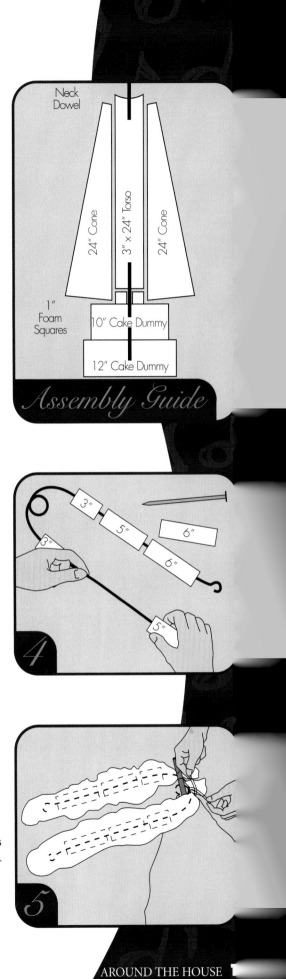

Assembly Guide

Neck Dowel
24" Cone
3" × 24" Torso
24" Cone
1" Foam Squares
10" Cake Dummy
12" Cake Dummy

4

5

DOORKNOB *Wreaths*

MATERIALS

- 18" (46 cm) medium-gauge wire
- 18" (46 cm) chenille stem
- 20 fresh leaves, 3" (7.5 cm) long x 1" (2.5 cm) wide, such as lemon leaf, laurel, camellia or bay (See Leaf Selection opposite)
- Hot glue gun
- Gold spray paint (optional)
- Matte acrylic spray finish (optional)
- 18" (46 cm) ribbon: satin, tulle or sheer
- Miscellaneous items: wire cutters, floral tape (optional), scissors, ruler, newspapers

Bring a little bit of Christmas into every room of your house with doorknob wreaths. Forgotten by many is the old custom of hanging miniature wreaths on every door; you can revive that tradition with a modern twist. Hot-gluing leaves to a wire form makes these wreaths a snap; leave them au naturel, or gild them with a coat of spray paint.

1 Leaf Selection: Check with your local florist for fresh leaves; they can give you price, availability and longevity recommendations. Salal, used here, more commonly known as lemon leaf, is one of the longest-lasting varieties and dries to a lovely sage green.

2 Wreath Form: Wrap the wire into a circle with a 5" (12.5 cm) diameter. Overlap the ends by 2½" (6.5 cm), twisting them around the wreath form. Wrap the chenille stem around the wreath form, as shown in the Step 2 illustration. Overlap the chenille stem ends in the same place on the wreath form as the wire ends overlap; this will be the top of the wreath.

3 Assembly: Hot-glue 1 leaf onto the wreath form where the wire ends overlap. Turn the wreath over, and hot-glue the leaf on the back side to help stabilize. Refer to the photo and the Step 3 illustration, overlapping the leaves halfway, or about 1½" (3.8 cm). Continue until the wreath form is completely covered.

4 Spraying: This is optional. To help preserve the wreaths for future use or current longevity, you may spray them with matte acrylic spray finish or gold spray paint. If you choose to leave your wreaths natural, move on to Step 5. Place newspapers in a well-ventilated area. Place wreath on newspapers, and spray with acrylic finish or gold paint, following manufacturer's instructions for usage and drying times. Spray the gold paint lightly, or completely for a gilded effect. Spray both the front and back sides; let dry at least 4 hours.

5 Bow: Tie ribbon into a 2-loop bow around the bottom of the wreath. Hang the wreath directly over the doorknob. This is the best option for doors that are opened and closed frequently.

6 Ribbon Hanger: Fold ribbon in half, and bring the center through the wreath at the top. Pull the ends through the center loop, cinching the ribbon gently up around the wreath as shown in the Step 6 illustration. Tie the ribbon ends together in a small bow and hang the wreath from the ribbon loop. This type of hanger is the best option for doors that remain open, so you don't accidentally shut the door on and crush the wreath.

7 Storing: These wreaths, if carefully stored, can last until the next season. They should be wrapped completely and placed so they will not be crushed, in a bug-free, dry environment. A fresh coat of paint or a new ribbon can spruce them up to look like new again. This method of wreath making can also be used for larger, full-size wreaths as well. Simply buy a larger wire form and many more leaves.

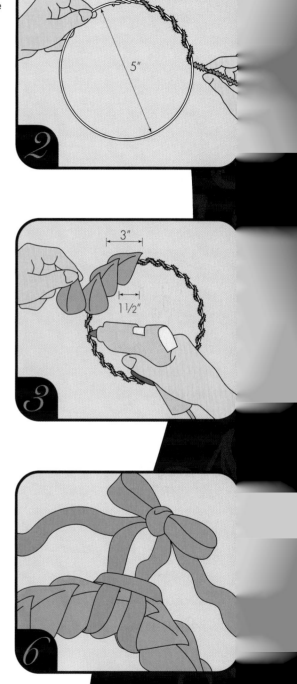

One-Horse
OPEN SLEIGH

Make this traditional winter scene to hang above your fireplace mantel while also staying within your holiday crafting budget! Save money by purchasing wool remnants from the fabric store or cutting the pattern pieces from second-hand wool clothing. Fuse each piece to the background, then neatly blanket-stitch the edges. Listen carefully and you just might hear sleigh bells jingling off in the distance.

MATERIALS

- Wool fabrics: two 7¼" x 8⅝" (18.7 x 22 cm) pieces medium blue for tree backgrounds, 8⅝" x 15¼" (22 x 38.7 cm) light gray for sleigh background, 5" x 8" (12.5 x 20.5 cm) dark green for trees and blanket, 4" x 6" (10 x 15 cm) brown for horse, 4" x 5" (10 x 12.5 cm) dark red for sleigh, 2½" x 5" (6.5 x 12.5 cm) black for sleigh runner, 2" x 4" (5 x 10 cm) navy for scarf, 1" (2.5 cm) square each beige for face and white for pom-pom, 1½" (3.8 cm) square blue for hat
- ⅓ yd. (0.32 m) paper-backed fusible web
- DMC No. 8 pearl cotton: 1 skein each in colors listed in Assembly Chart
- Embroidery needle
- Mounting board, 6⅝" x 23½" (16.5 x 59.8 cm)
- Wood frame, 6⅝" x 23½" (16.5 x 59.8 cm)
- Pattern Sheet
- Miscellaneous items: pencil, scissors, ruler, tracing paper, straight pins, lightweight cardboard, press cloth, steam iron, sewing machine and matching threads

1 Preparation: Follow manufacturer's instructions to fuse web to wrong side of all fabrics except backgrounds. Trace the patterns and cut from cardboard to make templates. Reverse templates and trace onto paper backing of fused fabrics; cut out.

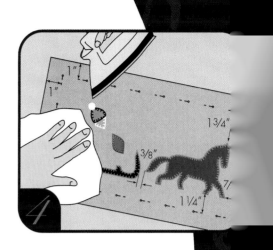

2 Background: Use a ruler and straight pins to mark a 1" (2.5 cm) border on all sides of the 3 background fabrics. Refer to the Assembly Guide for where to put sleigh, tree and horse pieces. Measurements show the distance from the 1" (2.5 cm) pinned borders.

3 Blanket-Stitching: See page 155 Embroidery Stitches for instructions on how to do the blanket stitch. To begin, do not knot thread, but hold a 2" (5 cm) tail on back until anchored by the first few stitches. To end, run thread under several stitches on back. Use 1 strand of pearl cotton to work 1/8" (3 mm) deep stitches evenly spaced every 1/8" to 3/16" (3 to 4.5 mm) around fabric edges. Where pieces overlap on the sleigh, blanket-stitch edge on top layer only.

4 Fusing: Fuse and blanket-stitch the pieces 1 at a time in the order given with the pearl cotton color listed in the Color Key. Refer to the Step 4 illustration to cover completed pieces with a press cloth when fusing a new piece to prevent scorching the fabric or snagging the thread.

5 Finishing: Refer to the photo and Assembly Guide to stitch the 3 panels, right sides together, using 1" (2.5 cm) seam allowances. Steam press the completed design and seams flat, making sure not to press too hard. Use the steam, rather than iron pressure. Mount on board and insert into frame.

COLOR KEY

Piece	Pearl Cotton Color	DMC #
Tree	Ecru	Ecru
Horse	Red Copper	919
Sleigh Runner	Dk. Pewter Gray	413
Lap Blanket	Med. Garnet	815
Face	Vy. Lt. Tan	738
Hat	Black	310
Pom-pom	Vy. Dk. Beige Gray	640
Sleigh	Ultra Vy. Dk. Topaz	780
Scarf	Ecru	Ecru

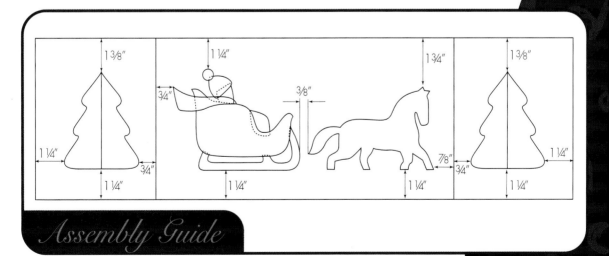

Assembly Guide

POINSETTIA
Print Tablecloth

Who would have thought you could even recycle your old poinsettia? This is the perfect project for after the holidays, allowing you to get a jump on next year's decorating or gifts. Simply painting the plucked poinsettia leaves, and pressing them, will create this stunning tablecloth sure to be the toast of the evening.

MATERIALS

- Cotton or linen tablecloth, size of your choice. 70" x 54" (178 x 137 cm) was used; natural fibers work the best for the printing process.
- Fabric paints: green, yellow, red, red-violet
- Colorless fabric paint extender
- Artists' paintbrushes: two 1" (2.5 cm) flat, ½" (1.3 cm) flat, liner
- Poinsettia plant; the larger the leaves, the faster the design can be painted, because they take up more room
- Atomizer or mister with water
- Newsprint sketchpad or paper towels
- Miscellaneous items: iron, old tablecloth or sheet, measuring tape, masking tape, freezer paper, tweezers, container for water, paint palette or mixing surface

1 Preparation: Wash and dry tablecloth as you will after use; press. Do not use any fabric softeners. Read Steps 3-5 and 7, and practice printing leaves on some scrap fabric; particularly experiment with varying the colors in the leaves. Lay tablecloth where it can remain undisturbed while painting. Slightly pad the work surface with an old tablecoth, sheet or layers of newsprint; paint may seep through the tablecloth.

2 Design Area: Measure tablecloth to find center, and mark with masking tape. Measure in 12" (30.5 cm) on each side, and mark 4 points with masking tape. See the Step 2 illustration to place additional pieces of tape around to mark out oval for center design area.

3 Painting: Mist the tablecloth center with water to make fabric more receptive to paint. Do not use a regular spray bottle; fabric will be too damp. Remove one of the smallest red inner poinsettia leaves; lay it on a piece of freezer paper facedown. See the Step 5 illustration to dip the 1" (2.5 cm) brush in red paint and paint the veiny underside of the leaf. Dip brush into paint exender randomly to thin the paint and add variety.

4 Printing: Refer to photo and the Step 2 illustration. Pick up the leaf with tweezers and place paint side down, close to center, stem in. Place newsprint or paper towel over the leaf. Use the palm of your hand to gently press down as shown in the Step 7 illustration. Do not move your hands, or you will move the leaf. Peel away the newsprint carefully; leave leaf in place.

5 First Ring: Remove center mark. Pick a new leaf and repeat Steps 3 and 4 to make a circle of leaves around the center. Slightly overlap the leaves, and mist them constantly to keep them from curling. Paint streaks of yellow or red-violet randomly on the leaves for shading and highlighting, as shown in the Step 5 illustration.

6 Red Leaves: Print the next rings with ever larger leaves, continuing to overlap leaves and the previous ring and to mist the leaves and the tablecloth. If you run out of red leaves, paint green leaves red. Make 4 curved rows on each side of the rings. Use larger and larger leaves, tapering to 1 or 2 leaves; at the outer edges, start to use some green paint. As soon as previous leaves no longer overlap, carefully remove them. Lay them aside, or mist them clean for reuse.

7 Green Leaves: Print a circle of green leaves in an oval encircling the red leaves; see Step 7 illustration. Use the other 1" (2.5 cm) brush in green paint, adding yellow, red, red violet and extender. Continue to print green leaves until you have filled in the entire oval. If you need to move the tablecloth to complete the design, let it dry first, or you may smear the design from the back.

8 Finishing: After printing, touch up any rough areas with the 1/2" (1.3 cm) paintbrush. Fill in any undesirable gaps with dark red or dark green. Refer to the poinsettia plant and use the liner brush to paint yellow dots in the center; add green highlight dots and randomly outline with red-violet. Print leaves scattered randomly over the rest of the tablecloth, covering up any paint spatters, if necessary. Refer to the fabric paint manufacturer's instructions to heat-set fabric paint. Launder as you did for preparation, and iron only on the reverse side.

Sophisticated SPHERES

Spheres are a popular design accent in home decor, and here's how you can create your own! Wrap foam balls in fresh eucalyptus leaves and gold trims—such as ribbons, wire, raffia, cord and beaded head pins—for texture and interest. Display the spheres on a bed of preserved cedar foliage accented with huckleberries for a Christmas centerpiece that goes beyond the traditional poinsettia with stunning style!

MATERIALS

- 6" x 11½" (15 x 29.3 cm) earthenware bowl in decorative stand
- Styrofoam® shapes: 3" (7.5 cm) foam disc; balls: one each 5" (12.5 cm); 3" (7.5 cm); 2½" (6.5 cm); two 4" (10 cm)
- 30 to 50 fresh silver dollar eucalyptus with 2" (5 cm) leaves
- Ten 12" (30.5 cm) stems preserved cedar
- Two 24" (61 cm) red/gold huckleberry sprays
- 5 pinecones 1" to 3" (2.5 to 7.5 cm)
- 2 oz. (50 g) Spanish moss
- Three 36" (91.5 cm) lengths natural raffia
- Assorted trims: ½ yd. (0.5 m) gold lace ribbon, 1" (2.5 cm) wide; 1 yd. (0.95 m)

- each: ³⁄₁₆" (4.5 mm) gold braid; ¾" (2 cm) ivory/gold chiffon wire-edge ribbon; 1¼ yd. (1.15 m) gold cord, ¹⁄₁₆" (1.5 mm) wide, ¾ yd. (0.7 m) 28-gauge gold bead wire
- 14 each gold beads: ½" (1.3 cm), ¼" (6 mm)
- Spray adhesive: lightweight, heavy-duty
- Clear acrylic spray
- White craft glue
- Four 4" (10 cm) wood floral picks
- Floral pins
- Miscellaneous items: kraft paper, serrated knife, cutting board, scissors, wire cutters, tape measure, straight pins

1 Preparation: Strip all of the leaves from the eucalyptus. Work outside or in a well-ventilated area; cover work surface with kraft paper. Follow manufacturer's instructions and spray the paper evenly with the lightweight adhesive. Wait 30 seconds, then press the eucalyptus leaves facedown into the tacky adhesive.

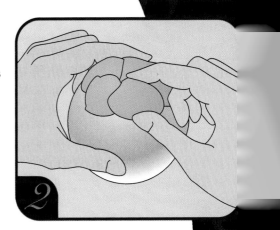

2 Gluing: Spray the leaves with the heavy-duty adhesive. Heavy-duty side down, press the leaves 1 at a time onto the largest foam ball; see Step 2 illustration. Instead of using spray adhesive, you may simply brush white craft glue onto the back of each leaf. Start at 1 end, overlapping leaves slightly, and work in rows around the ball until it is covered. Repeat for each ball except the 3" (7.5 cm); spray with acrylic sealer and let dry.

3 Decorating: Refer to the photo to decorate the spheres. Pin or use white craft glue to anchor the trims, then wrap them, pinning and gluing at various points to secure. When dry, insert a wood pick halfway into the center bottom of each sphere.

4 5" (12.5 cm) Sphere: Wrap the 3/16" (4.5 mm) gold braid around the sphere, then the chiffon ribbon, letting it twist occasionally.

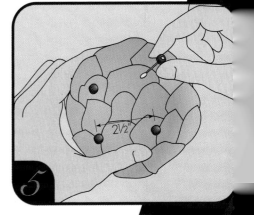

5 4" (10 cm) Spheres: Wrap 1 sphere with raffia, then with a 3/4-yd. (0.7 m) length of 1/16" (1.5 mm) gold cord. For the remaining 4" (10 cm) sphere, string each gold bead on a straight pin, dip the pin into glue and insert it into the sphere. Refer to the Step 5 illustration to pin the 1/2" (1.3 cm) beads 2 1/2" (6.5 cm) apart, then pin the 1/4" (6 mm) beads halfway between the larger ones. Wrap the remaining 1/16" (1.5 mm) gold cord randomly around the sphere.

6 2 1/2" (6.5 cm) Sphere: Glue the lace ribbon around the center of the sphere horizontally, then glue a second length vertically, dividing the sphere into 4 equal sections. Wrap with gold bead wire to finish.

7 Foam Base: Use the serrated knife to cut the 3" (7.5 cm) foam ball in half. Glue 1 half centered on the foam disc; place flat side up in the bowl. Cover with Spanish moss and secure with floral pins.

8 Centerpiece Greens: Cut twenty-four 3" to 6" (7.5 to 15 cm) lengths from the cedar foliage. See the Step 8 illustration to insert the stems around the outer edge of the foam, creating a "collar." Cut the huckleberry sprays into eight 3" to 6" (7.5 to 15 cm) lengths. Insert stems nestled in the cedar. Arrange the spheres in the bowl, inserting the opposite end of the picks into the foam. Arrange pinecones among the spheres as desired.

Saint NICHOLAS

St. Nicholas, dressed in his splendid robes and miter, is laden with a bag of toys and carries a Christmas tree and staff to bring the spirit of Christmas to us all. The basic figure crafted from foam eggs and wire is costumed in paper twist with fleece trim. Add St. Nicholas to your Christmas figure collection and make several for gifts, too.

MATERIALS

- Paper twist: 10 yd. (9.15 m) ivory, 7½" (19.3 cm) wide; ½ yd. (0.5 m) peach, 4" (10 cm) wide
- 2" (5 cm) Styrofoam® eggs, two
- Wire: 21" (53.5 cm) of 18-gauge; white spool of 28-gauge
- ⅜" (1 cm) wood dowel, 10" (25.5 cm)
- 6" x 12" (15 x 30.5 cm) acrylic lamb's wool
- Platinum doll hair
- 27" (68.5 cm) wired ivory satin cord
- Assorted miniature toys and packages
- 4" (10 cm) flocked brush tree
- Polyester fiberfill
- Metallic gold marker
- Acrylic paints: pink, gold
- ¼" (6 mm) flat paintbrush
- 4-oz. (125 g) bottle thick white craft glue
- Yellow transfer paper
- Pattern Sheet
- Miscellaneous items: straight pins, pencil, scissors, ruler, tracing paper, wire cutters, black and blue fine-point permanent-ink markers, paint palette

1 Preparation: Untwist all paper twist, and cut the following: from peach twist: 6" (15 cm) for head, ½" (1.3 cm) for neck and two 6" (15 cm) lengths for arms; from ivory twist: twelve 18" (46 cm) lengths for skirt, 24" (61 cm) for coat and 6" x 7½" (15 x 19.3 cm) for bag. Trace the patterns to tracing paper and cut out from ivory twist. Cut lamb's wool into 1" (2.5 cm) strips. Paint dowel gold; let dry.

2 Head: Cut 10" (25.5 cm) of 18-gauge wire. Dip 1 end into glue and insert 1" (2.5 cm) into pointed end of 1 egg; see Step 2 illustration. Split head twist lengthwise and wrap 1 piece over egg, twisting at top. Wrap second piece, overlapping the first, and glue and smooth edges. Wire paper ends at bottom of egg with white wire and trim. Wrap neck twist around wired area to form neck.

3 Torso and Arms: Apply glue to wire 1″ (2.5 cm) below head. Insert wire through center of wide end of second egg, slide egg up to neck. Cut 11″ (28 cm) of 18-gauge wire. See the Step 2 illustration to push horizontally through torso egg, ¼″ (6 mm) below neck. Apply glue along 1 long edge of each sleeve twist piece, lay along arm wire, fold end in, wrap around wire, and glue.

4 Skirt and Sleeves: Wrap 12 skirt twist pieces, 1 at a time, around glue bottle to shape skirt. See the Step 4 illustration to use white wire around the center. Remove glue bottle and bend top down toward bottom. Pull outer layers to make bottom edges even; trim. Insert and glue torso wire into center skirt top until torso sits on top of skirt. Fold and glue a ½″ (1.3 cm) hem on sleeve twist pieces. Glue underarm seams together, slide sleeve up arm and glue to shoulder.

5 Apron: Use transfer paper and pencil to transfer border and large triangles to twist. Trace entire pattern with metallic gold marker. Refer to the photo to fill design with squiggles. Let dry. Glue apron to St. Nicholas' front at shoulder and side seams.

6 Coat: Fold coat twist in half widthwise, then fold in half lengthwise. Cut a neckline at folded corner and slit front edge only open; see Step 6 illustration. Place coat over shoulders with slit at front and glue side seams together. Glue a pleat at each shoulder. Glue lamb's wool strips to coat front edge and sleeves.

7 Face: See the Step 7 illustration to paint the face. Use black marker to draw eyes, nose and mouth. Draw eyes with blue marker. Thin pink paint with water and make 3 crescent strokes for cheeks and nose. Cut 4″ (10 cm) of doll hair and pull apart to fluff. Refer to photo to apply glue to head and lower face. Press hair into glue for hair, beard and mustache.

8 Hat: Glue 2 sets of 2 pieces together for front and back. See photo to outline hat and make squiggles with gold marker. Let dry. Glue front and back together along edges. Glue a lamb's wool strip around bottom; let dry. Place on head and secure with straight pins.

9 Bag: Fold bag twist in half. Gather and wire 1 end; turn. Overlap and glue sides together. Glue a wool strip around top edge; let dry. Lightly stuff with fiberfill. Knot ends of satin cord; fold in half and twist together 6″ (15 cm) from ends. Wrap ends around bag below lamb's wool and twist together. Glue toys and packages in bag opening. Loop cord over left shoulder, and glue. Glue bag to left side of coat, staff to left hand and tree to right hand.

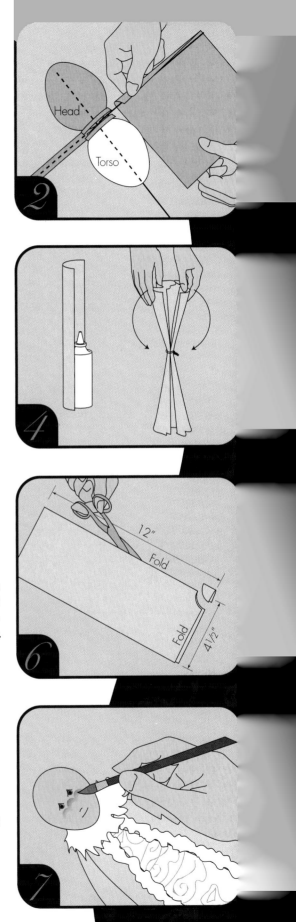

Mantel PENDULUM CLOCK

Don't let time get the better of you—make a special mantel clock just for Christmas. Created from a rough-hewn planter box, this clock will fit in well with country or folk art decor. The face only looks difficult to do. The circle was painted and outlined with a marker; the numerals are stickers. Self-adhesive clock faces are available that would make the job even easier—simply peel and stick!

MATERIALS

- 6" (15 cm) square wooden planter box*
- Drill with 3/8" drill bit
- Artist's brush: fine liner, 1" (2.5 cm) sponge
- Acrylic craft paints: pale green, buttercrunch, metallic gold
- 3/4" (2 cm) wide masking tape
- Fine-point black marking pen
- Purchased self-adhesive numbers, 24 pt.
- 12" (30.5 cm) gold pendulum, 2¾" (7 cm) diameter movement and hands*
- Pattern Sheet
- Miscellaneous items: ruler, pencil, fine sandpaper, scissors, old credit card, paint palette, tracing and transfer or graphite paper
- *(See Sources on page 159 for purchasing information.)

1 Preparation: Look over the planter box, and select the best side to use as the clock face. Use ruler to find the center of the clock face, and mark with a pencil; drill a 3/8" (1 cm) hole for clock movement. See the Step 1 illustration to wrap a scrap of sandpaper around a pencil and insert into the hole to sand and make it smooth. You may also use a rat-tail file, if you have one.

2 Painting: Refer to page 156 for Painting Instructions and Techniques. Basecoat the entire planter box, inside and out, with pale green paint using a 1" (2.5 cm) sponge brush. Let dry; apply another coat for complete coverage, if desired.

3 Side Stripes: Refer to the Step 3 illustration to put pieces of 3/4" (2 cm) masking tape every other 3/4" (2 cm) on both planter box sides. Use a credit card to rub along the masking tape edges to make sure it adheres well and the paint won't seep under. Use the sponge brush to paint the untaped areas with metallic gold paint. Remove tape, and let dry.

4 Clock Interior: Use the sponge brush to paint the inside of the box, side edges of the bottom, and top edges of the box sides with metallic gold paint; let dry.

5 Pattern: Trace the clock pattern to tracing paper. Cut out, and use graphite or transfer paper to transfer to the clock face, except for the Roman numerals. Center the pattern over the drilled hole. If you are going to use a self-adhesive clock face, transfer only the corner decorations.

6 Clock Face: Use the sponge brush to paint the face circle with buttercrunch paint. Let dry. Use the black marker to outline the face, making the outer ring. Make the inner ring and the dividing lines between the rings; refer to the Step 6 illustration. Follow the manufacturer's instructions to rub on the Roman numeral stickers in the appropriate places at the bold lines drawn between the 2 rings. For the self-adhesive clock face, peel off the paper and adhere it to the clock with the center hole over the drilled hole.

7 Finishing: Use the liner brush and metallic gold paint to outline the outer clock face ring, and add the corner decorations. Follow the manufacturer's instructions to install the clock movement and hands, and attach the pendulum.

Holiday DINING

Serving meals on these whimsical quilted tree placemats, complete with a tree trunk that holds napkins, will set the mood for a delightful dining experience. Strip quilting makes it quick and easy to stitch up as many table settings as needed. Use fabrics that are red and green, as shown , or make them sage green and gold for a contemporary look, mauve and burgundy for Victorian tastes.

MATERIALS

For 4 Placemats and Napkins
- 45" (115 cm) cotton fabrics:
- 2 yd. (1.85 m) red for centers, backing and napkins
- ¼ yd. (0.25 m) Fabric 1 dk. green print
- ½ yd. (0.5 m) Fabric 2 lt. green print
- ⅔ yd. (0.63 m) Fabric 3 dk. green print
- 1 yd. (0.95 m) low-loft quilt batting
- 3 pkgs. red extra-wide double-fold bias tape
- Rotary cutter and mat
- Transparent ruler with 60° marking
- Miscellaneous items: tracing paper, pencil, scissors, ruler, sewing needle, sewing machine and matching threads, iron, safety pins

1 Preparation: Prewash, dry and iron all fabrics. Stitch all seams ¼" (6 mm), right sides together, unless otherwise directed. See the Step 1 illustration to make the center triangle pattern on tracing paper. Use the transparent ruler with 60° marking to draw the lines, making a 6" (15 cm) equal-sided triangle. Make a 6" (15 cm) line for the base, and then place the ruler on both sides of the base to draw the other 2 lines. Measure all the lines to make sure they are each 6" (15 cm) long. Adjust if they are not equal, and cut out the pattern.

2 Cutting Fabrics: Cut 4 center triangles from red fabric along the 45" (115 cm) edge, and four 18" (46 cm) squares for napkins along the 2 yd. (1.85 m) selvage edge. The remaining fabric will be used for the placemat backings. Cut four 6" x 8" (15 x 20.5 cm) pieces from Fabric 3 for the tree trunks. Use the rotary cutter and ruler to cut the remaining Fabric 3, and all of Fabrics 1 and 2 into 2" x 45" (5 x 115 cm) strips.

3 Round 1: Refer to the Step 3 and 4 illustrations to place a Fabric 1 strip on 1 edge of a red center triangle, with at least 2″ (5 cm) extending on both sides. Stitch, and press seam away from the center triangle. Trim both ends, as shown in 3A, using the 60° angle line on transparent ruler, to match triangle. Stitch another Fabric 1 strip on the center triangle and the first strip, going around the triangle counter-clockwise; see 3B. Press, and trim at 60° angle as before. See 3C to stitch the last strip; press, and trim at 60° angle. The triangle should measure 11″ (28 cm) on each side.

4 Rounds 2 and 3: Continue sewing on fabric strips as done in Step 3, referring to the photo and the Step 4 illustration. The middle round uses Fabric 2, and the outer is done in Fabric 3. Begin each round of fabric strips on the same side of the triangle as done on the first round. Triangle should measure 16.5″ (41.8 cm) after Round 2, and 22″ (56 cm) after Round 3.

5 Cutting Layers: Place the placemat top on batting, and trace a line 1″ (2.5 cm) larger all around. Repeat to trace 4 layers; cut out. Repeat on the red fabric, to make 4 backing pieces. Place the backing on flat work surface, wrong side up. Place the batting, and then the placemat top, right side up. Baste layers together with safety pins.

6 Quilting: Quilt by machine or hand; begin stitching around the red triangle center. Use the stitch-in-the-ditch quilting technique, hiding the stitching in the seams. Continue around the 2 other triangle seams, stopping and fastening thread between each triangle round. Trim the outer edges even.

7 Trunk: Fold the trunk lengthwise into a 3″ x 8″ (7.5 x 20.5 cm) piece, right sides together. Stitch a seam along the 8″ (20.5 cm) edge; turn to right side, and press. Fold the short edges together. Pin to the back side of 1 outside edge of triangle placemat, centering on the edge and matching raw edges.

8 Binding: Place bias tape on wrong side of placemat, matching raw edges. Pin, and stitch along first bias tape foldline. Fold the tape to the front, mitering at corners. Pin, and stitch.

9 Napkins: Turn under ⅜″ (1 cm) along each side of napkin, stitch, and press. Repeat for a double hem. On last hem, use a machine or hand decorative embroidery stitch done in contrasting or metallic thread. Fold napkin twice lengthwise, flap down the tree trunk loop and insert through as shown in photo.

Gold-Trimmed
VELVET
STOCKINGS

*Follow the
instructions to
make these scrumptious stockings,
or find them ready-made and
just do the fun-and-easy part of decorating.
Add braid, tassels, fringe, and painted wooden
cutouts—available in a variety of designs. If
you are really in a rush, don't even bother stitching; use self-adhesive cutouts, and stick them on.*

ALL STOCKINGS

1 Pattern: For purchased stockings, follow Step 3 to decorate. Use a stocking that you already have for pattern; trace on tracing paper. For the Heart Stocking, draw a line across stocking pattern at cuff, and cut. Add 1/2" (1.3 cm) seam allowance around all patterns; see the Step 1 illustration. Add 1 1/2" (3.8 cm) to the top of Heart Stocking cuffs for hems; cut out patterns.

2 Velvet/Tapestry Fabrics: Refer to the Step 2 illustration to lay out the patterns, and cut out a front and back, and cuffs, if applicable. Velvet and tapestries are slippery, napped fabrics; cut them a single layer at a time. Stitch all seams 1/2" (1.3 cm), right sides together; finger-press seams.

3 Wooden Cutouts: Basecoat the front side with metallic gold and sponge brush; do not paint back or edges. Let dry; add another coat, if desired. Drill 1/16" (1.5 mm) holes in the cutouts, referring to the photo. Place cutouts on the stocking as desired. Brush fabric glue onto the back, and adhere. Let dry. It is not necessary to stitch on the cutouts after gluing, but it adds another decorative touch. Thread the sewing needle with 18" (46 cm) of metallic thread. Stitch cutouts through drilled holes as shown in the photo.

JOY STOCKING

1 Assembly: Take cuff width measurement, and cut 2 each front and back cuffs, 2" (5 cm) long. Pin front cuff to front stocking, and back cuff to back stocking; stitch. Baste the tassel to the right side of the back stocking on the stocking/cuff seams; pin front and back pieces with the tassel sandwiched. See the Heart Stocking illustration to stitch the sides and bottom together. Clip curves; trim seams at points.

2 Cuff: Stitch the remaining cuff pieces along the short edges to make a continuous loop. Turn under a scant 1/4" (6 mm) along 1 long edge and hem. Place the loop cuff over the stocking cuff, matching the unhemmed long edge and seams. Pin, and stitch. Turn loop cuff to the inside; press along seam. Hand-stitch inner cuff along hem to outer cuff at seams. Fold hanging loop cord in half, and hand-stitch the ends together for 1" (2.5 cm); stitch loop to the inside of the cuff along the left seam.

FLEUR-DE-LIS STOCKING

Repeat Step 1 of Joy Stocking, cutting cuffs 3" (7.5 cm) long and basting tassel at toe. Measure around stocking top and cut fringe; add 1/2" (1.3 cm) for overlap. Pin and stitch to stocking, right below cuff, over-lapping in back. Repeat for gold braid. Follow Step 2 of Joy Stocking to finish cuff; finish hanging loop as follows. Fold hanging loop cord in half, and tie an overhand knot 1 1/2" (3.8 cm) from end. Hand-stitch loop to outside of stocking.

HEART STOCKING

Follow Step 1 of Joy Stocking to assemble, ignoring the first sentence and basting tassel at toe. Fold 1 1/2" (3.8 cm) hem on cuff to wrong side. Finger-press, and pin. Follow Fleur-de-Lis Stocking to measure, and pin the gold braid 1 1/4" (3.2 cm) below the top. Stitch braid, catching in the hem at the same time.

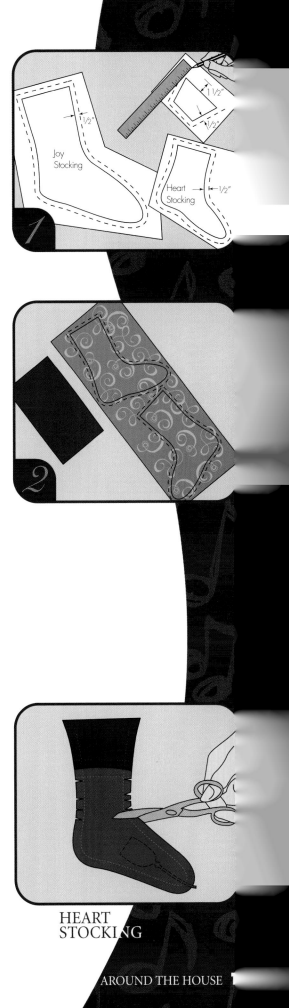

HEART
STOCKING

ENTRYWAY
Elegance

The front door sets the tone for Christmas. A kissing ring with a sprig of mistletoe nestled within will encourage holiday smooches when hung in the entryway. A handsome swag built on a brass horn simply trimmed with greens, berries and abundant gold and burgundy ribbons heralds the holidays.

MATERIALS

For Both Projects
- 26-gauge wire

For Kissing Ring
- 10" (25.5 cm) artificial pine wreath
- Artificial mistletoe sprig
- 9 pinecones, 2" to 3" (5 to 7.5 cm)
- 5 berry sprays
- 6 yd. (5.5 m) each ¼" to ⅜" (6 mm to 1 cm) wide ribbon: red lamé, gold sheer
- 2½ yd. (2.3 m) gold sheer ribbon, 1½" (3.8 cm) wide
- Green floral tape

For Brass Horn Swag
- 21" (53.5 cm) brass French horn
- 34" (86.5 cm) artificial blue spruce swag
- 2 yd. (1.85 m) wired burgundy velvet ribbon, 2½" (6.5 cm) wide
- 3 yd. (2.75 m) gold/burgundy ribbon, 1½" (3.8 cm) wide
- 2 red berry sprays
- Miscellaneous items: scissors, wire cutters, ruler

KISSING RING

1 Pinecone/Berry Clusters: Use floral wire and tape to make 3 berry spray/pinecone clusters. Refer to photo to wire clusters to outside of wreath.

2 Bows: Refer to the Brass Horn Swag illustration to make bows. Cut the 1½" (3.8 cm) gold ribbon in half, and tie 2 multiloop bows; wire to 2 of the pinecone/berry clusters. Cut four 1-yd. (0.95 m) lengths each of the red lamé and gold sheer ribbons. Make 4 multiloop bows, each from a red and gold ribbon length; wire 2 between 2 of the pinecone/berry clusters.

3 Hanger: Cut 27" (68.5 cm) of red ribbon, and fold in half. Make a knot in the center to form a 2½" (6.5 cm) hanging loop. Cut remaining 2 yd. (1.85 m) of gold ribbon into 4 equal 18" (46 cm) lengths. Evenly space them, and tie to the wreath; see the Kissing Ring illustration. Take 2 opposite gold ribbon lengths, match the ends, and tie in an overhand knot at the red ribbon knot. Repeat for the other 2 ribbons; trim all ends close to knot. Wire remaining 2 red/gold ribbon bows to hanging loop knot.

4 Mistletoe: Tie stem of mistletoe sprig to hanging end of red ribbon. Use remaining red ribbon to tie a bow on the mistletoe.

KISSING RING

BRASS HORN SWAG

1 Bows: Refer to the Brass Horn Swag illustration to make bows by looping ribbon from side to side. Hold ribbon in the bow center and pinch; wrap loops tightly with wire. Make a bow from 2 yd. (1.85 m) of gold/ burgundy ribbon with ten 2½" (6.5 cm) loops, a small center loop and 3 streamers—12", 10" and 9" (30.5, 25.5 and 23 cm) long. Make a 4-loop bow from wired velvet ribbon with two 4½" (11.5 cm) top loops and two 5½" (14 cm) bottom loops. Use remaining ribbon for 2 streamers. Wire gold/burgundy bow to the center of velvet bow.

2 Assembly: Wire the horn to center of the spruce swag with horn and mouthpiece at the top. Shape swag to the curve of the horn and bend branches to make swag appear fuller. Overlap berry stem ends and wire stems to the center of the swag. Separate berries to give a fuller look; wire where necessary.

3 Finishing: Fold the remaining yd. (0.95 m) of gold/burgundy ribbon in half and wire center of ribbon to top center of horn. Wire bow on top of ribbon to horn in the same place, forming a circular wire hanger on back of swag at the same time. Refer to the photo to tuck ribbons among greens.

BRASS HORN SWAG

So-o-o Big Snowman
FOOTSTOOL

Most snowmen like the cold, but this irresistible snowman enjoys the warmth of a holiday home. And who won't get a chuckle when they see this painted footstool? Thank goodness he's a no-melt fellow, otherwise you can imagine the puddle he'd become!

MATERIALS

- Unfinished wood footstool, 9" x 11" x 6¼" (23 x 28 x 15.7 cm)
- Acrylic paints: black, brown, Christmas red, white, orange, midnight blue, Salem blue, Victorian blue
- Paintbrushes: 1" (2.5 cm) sponge, No. 3 round, fine liner, small flat, small stencil
- Matte acrylic spray varnish
- Pattern Sheet
- Miscellaneous items: tracing and graphite paper, pencil, disposable palette, brush basin, plastic wrap, paper towels

1 Basecoat: See page 156 for Painting Instructions and Techniques. Use the sponge brush to basecoat the footstool, except for the top, with Salem blue; let dry. Mix midnight blue with an equal amount of water. Brush thinned paint over a small patch of the Salem blue basecoat, then dab the wet paint with a crumpled ball of plastic wrap to produce a textured look. Repeat over the entire painted part of the footstool, working small areas at a time.

2 Sky: Trace the painting pattern onto tracing paper. Use the graphite paper and pencil to transfer the pattern to the top of the stool. Use the flat brush to basecoat the sky with Victorian blue, extending color onto the footstool edges; see the Step 2 illustration. Let dry, then dry-brush lower sky with Salem blue, working from the horizon up.

3 Snowman & Snow: Use the flat brush to basecoat the snowman and snow with white, extending the color onto the footstool edges. Paint the twig arms brown, then use the liner brush and white to highlight the top of each arm.

4 Face: Use the liner brush to paint the nose orange, and then use red to paint the carrot lines and shade the bottom. To shade, use the liner brush to paint the area, then dip the round brush in water to quickly blend and pull the paint out. Paint black dots for the coal eyes, mouth and buttons. Dot each with a tiny white highlight. Paint a thin Salem blue line around the top of each coal piece.

5 Snow Shading: Shade lines under the snowman head, tummy and base first with Salem blue, then randomly with midnight blue. Repeat to shade areas where the twig arms meet the snow body; see the Step 5 illustration.

6 Snow Coloring: Dip the stencil brush in red paint and use the dry-brush technique to rouge snowman cheeks. Repeat to randomly rouge the snowman and the snow underneath with Salem and Victorian blue.

7 Snowflakes: See the Step 7 illustration to use end of an artist's brush in white paint to make ³/₁₆" (4.5 m) dot snowflakes close together to fill the sky.

8 Sky Shading: Shade the sky around the snowman with Victorian blue. Dry-brush the footstool top edges as follows: snow with Salem blue, and sky halfway down the sides with midnight blue. Let dry, then spray with several light coats of varnish.

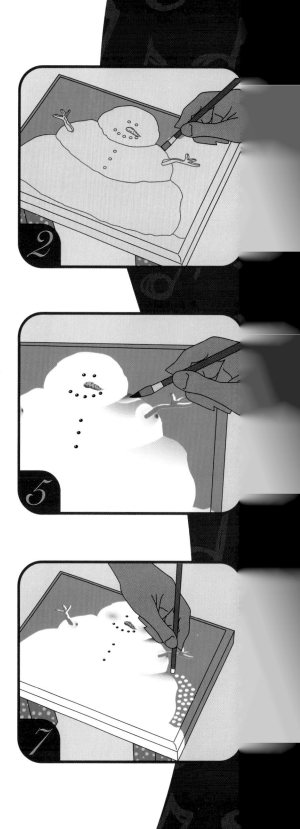

Burgundy BOW DUO

Burgundy bows abound on the crocheted tree skirt and afghan. What a warm and welcome way to decorate for the holidays with the pentagon-shaped skirt and matching afghan. The bow border is cross-stitched on with yarn after all the crocheting is complete.

MATERIALS

- 7 skeins each 100 gr. worsted-weight yarn: (A) off-white, (B) burgundy, (C) green
- Size J crochet hook
- No. 16 tapestry needle
- Scissors

PREPARATION

Refer to page 154 for Crochet Abbreviations and Stitches. When changing colors, always work last pull through of color being worked with color to be worked.
Gauge: 15 sc = 4" (10 cm)
16 dc = 4" (10 cm)
Afghan: 48" x 60" (122 x 152.5 cm)
Tree Skirt: 48" (122 cm)

AFGHAN

1 Body: Ch 176 with A yarn and J crochet hook.
Row 1: Sc in 2nd ch from hook and in each ch across, 175 sc worked, turn.
Rows 2-24: Ch 1, sc in each sc across, turn. At end of Row 24, end off.
Row 25: Attach C in 21st sc from edge, ch 3 (counts as dc), dc in next 4 sc, *with B, dc in next 5 sc; with C, dc in next 5 sc; rep from * across leaving 20 sc at end, turn—135 dc.
Row 26: With C, ch 3, dc in next 4 dc, *with B, dc in next 5 dc; with C, dc in next 5 dc; rep from * ending with C, dc in last 4 dc and in top of ch 3. Rep Row 26 until afghan measures 53" (134.5 cm) from the beginning. End off.

2 Side Bands: Join A to either side left unstitched.
Row 1: Ch 1, sc in each sc across, turn—20 sc.
Rows 2-24: Rep Row 1. End off at end of first side. To work second side, join A and rep Rows 1-24; do not end off at end of Row 24, turn.

3 Bottom Band:
Row 1: With A, ch 1, sc across 20 sc just worked, sc across the next 135 dc, sc across last 20 sc, turn—175 sc.
Rows 2-24: Ch 1, sc across, turn. End off.

4 Border: Join C to corner.
Row 1: Ch 3, dc in next dc and around, working 3 dc in each corner, ending with 2 dc in same sc as beg ch 3. End off.
Row 2: To make the scalloped edge, join B in corner, ch 4, work (dc, hdc, sc) in next dc; *sk 2 dc, sc in next dc, sk 2 dc, in next dc work (sc, hdc, dc, tr, dc, hdc, sc)—cluster worked; rep from * across ending with half cluster (sc, hdc, dc, tr), sl st to beg ch 4.

5 Finishing: Sew side bands to body. Block with damp cloth and iron. Cross-stitch the bows on border following the Stitch Chart. Center a bow on each side and repeat, working out to each corner.

TREE SKIRT

1 Ch 53 with C yarn and J crochet hook, beginning in the center and working out.

Row 1: Dc in 4th ch from hook and in next ch (counts as 3 dc), *with B, dc in next 5 ch; with C, dc in next 5 ch; rep from * ending with C, dc in last 3 ch, turn.

Row 2: With C, ch 3, dc in same dc as ch 3 (inc made), dc in next 2 dc, *with B, dc in next 5 dc; with C, dc in next 2 dc, 5 dc in next dc (5 dc inc), dc in next 2 dc; rep from * ending with C, dc in next 2 dc, 2 dc in last dc, turn.

Row 3: With C, ch 3, inc 1 dc, work dc's across keeping colors as established. Work a 5 dc inc in the 3rd dc of each 5 dc inc from previous row, ending with C, dc in each dc to last one, inc 1 in last dc.

Row 4: With B, ch 3, inc 1 dc, work dc's across keeping colors as established. Work a 5 dc inc in the 3rd dc of each 5 dc inc from previous row, ending with C on 5 dc's, with B, 2 dc in last dc, turn.

Row 5: With B, ch 3, inc 1 dc, work as in Row 5, ending with B, dc to last dc, inc 1 dc in last dc, turn.

Rows 6-7: Rep Row 5.

Rows 8-12: Rep Row 3.

Rows 13-17: Rep Row 5.

Rows 18-22: Rep Row 3.

Rows 23-27: Rep Row 5.

Row 28: Rep Row 3.

2 Bottom Band:

Row 1: With A, ch 1, 2 sc in first dc (sc inc), sc across working 3 sc in 3rd dc of 5 dc inc of previous row, ending with 2 sc in last dc, turn.

Row 2: Ch 1, sc in each sc across, turn.

Rows 3-16: Rep Rows 1-2. End off.

3 Border:

Row 1: With C, ch 3, dc across, working 5 dc inc in 3rd dc of each 5 dc inc in previous row. End off.

Row 2: Repeat Row 2 of AFGHAN Border, omitting the last sl st.

4 Tie Bands: With B, ch 1, work 2 rows sc along back opening. Ch 40 for the top tie; end off. Attach B 7" (18 cm) below previous tie, ch 40 for the second and third ties; end off. Repeat for second back opening.

5 Finishing: Cross-stitch the bows on border following the Stitch Chart. Center a bow on each side and repeat, working out to each corner.

Color Key
x Burgundy
• Green

LACE-LOOK *Stocking*

Cross-stitching a heart and snowflake design with white embroidery floss on red Aida cloth creates the elegant appearance of lace appliqués. A row of these on the mantel for every family member is sure to brighten any home for the holidays.

1 Stitching: Refer to the Cross-Stitch General Instructions and Stitches on page 155 and the Stitch Chart on the Pattern Sheet to stitch the design with 2 strands of floss. Use a pencil to draw desired name in space at top of stocking chart. Backstitch name centered between top rows of lace design. Sew a white basting stitch around stocking outline at edge of stitched design.

2 Stocking: Cut Aida stocking shape ½" (1.3 cm) from basted outline. See the Step 2 illustration to use the stocking as a pattern and cut 2 lining pieces from white fabric and 1 backing piece from red/white miniprint, reversing the backing and 1 lining piece.

3 Assembly: Sew all pieces with right sides together, using a ½" (1.3 cm) seam allowance. Pin and sew Aida and backing together, leaving top open. Trim seam, clip curves and turn. Turn ½" (1.3 cm) around top edge to inside and press. Sew lining pieces, leaving top edge open. Turn ½" (1.3 cm) of top edge to outside and press. Insert lining in stocking.

4 Hanger: Cut a 6" (15 cm) piece of ribbon and fold in half. Insert cut ends between lining and backing at top back seam. Tack ribbon in place and slipstitch lining to stocking top.

MATERIALS

- 14-count red Aida cloth, 15" x 21" (38 x 53.5 cm)
- White embroidery floss
- No. 24 tapestry needle
- 45" (115 cm) cotton fabric, ½ yd. (0.5 m) each: red/white miniprint; white
- Red sewing thread
- ¼ yd. (0.25 m) white grosgrain ribbon, ⅝" (1.5 cm) wide
- Pattern Sheet
- Miscellaneous items: sewing needle, scissors, straight pins, pencil, sewing matchine, iron

Canine Christmas
COUNTDOWN

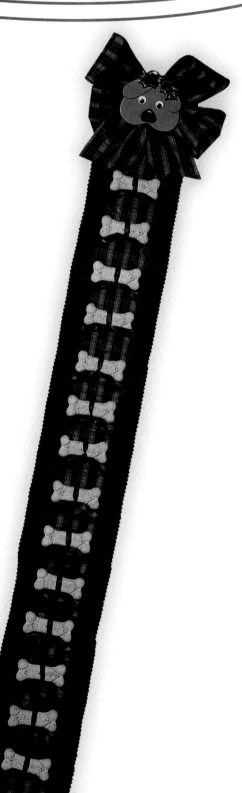

Tie treats to the bellpull and Fido will have a tail-waggin' good time until Santa comes. Felt, with its no-finish edges, makes an easy base on which to stitch ribbon. The dog face is made from purchased wooden hearts, and craft sticks cut for ears. If you are of the feline persuasion, use the cat pattern and tie up kitty treats.

MATERIALS

- ⅓ yd. (0.32 m) red felt, 36" (91.5 cm) wide
- Ribbon: 3 yd. (2.75 m) red/green plaid, 3" (7.5 cm) wide; 3 yd. (2.75 m) red satin, ¼" (6 mm) wide; ½ yd. (0.5 m) red satin, ⅛" (3 mm) wide
- 14 dog biscuits for small to medium dogs
- Wood hearts: 3" (7.5 cm), 1" (2.5 cm)
- Acrylic paints: raw sienna, black, white
- Small flat paintbrush
- 10 mm wiggle eyes, two
- Mini holly sprig
- 6 mm gold jingle bell
- Jumbo craft stick
- Hot glue gun
- Miscellaneous items: scissors, pinking shears, craft knife, ruler, straight pins, sewing machine, red sewing thread, sewing needle, water container, dressmaker's chalk, 24-gauge floral wire

1 Base: Fold felt in half to make a 6" x 36" (15 x 91.5 cm) strip; pin edges. Begin at 1 end of felt, and center plaid ribbon width-wise; pin. Topstitch close to ribbon edges. Use chalk to mark felt 1" (2.5 cm) from ribbon on long edges. See the Step 1 illustration to trim on chalk lines, with pinking shears, and along top and bottom edges, cutting off ribbon at the bottom edge.

2 Face: Refer to the pattern to trace ears and cut from jumbo craft stick with craft or utility knife. Use the flat paintbrush to paint large heart and ears with raw sienna. Paint small heart black; highlight with white, referring to the pattern and photo. Refer to the pattern to hot-glue ears, eyes and small heart nose to large heart head. Tie 1/8" (3 mm) red ribbon into a small bow. Hot-glue bow to holly sprig, and holly sprig and jingle bell to top of head.

3 Treat Holders: Cut 1/4" (6 mm) red ribbon into fourteen 7" (18 cm) lengths. Center on plaid ribbon at 2" (5 cm) intervals; pin. Tack stitch each at center; see the Step 3 illustration.

4 Assembly: Make remaining plaid ribbon into a 4-loop bow; wrap wire tightly around the center to secure. Hot-glue bow to top of wall hanging. Glue puppy head to bow center. Tack remaining 1/4" (6 mm) into a ribbon loop to top back center for hanger. Tie a dog biscuit on each ribbon.

DOG PATTERN

CAT PATTERN

OTHER VERSIONS

Make the cat head, painting it the colors of your favorite feline—Siamese, calico or Halloween black. You could also make a child's version by painting hearts skin-tone and coloring the craft-stick hair; tie up candy canes or other Christmas goodies. To make a true Advent calendar, purchase 5 1/4 yd. (4.8 m) of 1/4" (6 mm) red ribbon, instead of 3 yd. (2.75 m). Cut twenty-five 7" (18 cm) lengths, and tack on, centered at 1" (2.5 cm) intervals, beginning 3" (7.5 cm) from the bottom.

DE-LIGHTFUL *Basket*

Christmas is indeed the season of lights, and with the shorter days, we all look for ways to brighten up our homes. Here is a way to combine fresh greens with lights, making a wonderful floral arrangement. Display against a wall near an outlet source, or use lights that come with a battery pack, and place the basket on a dining room or coffee table for a spectacular centerpiece.

1 Greens: Many varieties of greens are available in your own backyard, at Christmas tree farms or from your local florist. Some of the possibilities are: pine, balsam, eucalyptus, ming fern, boxwood, seeded eucalyptus and camellia. Separate and cut the greens into 8" to 9" (20.5 to 23 cm) lengths.

2 Basket: Put in basket liner; liners are available from your local florist or craft store. Soak floral foam in the sink for 30 minutes. Use serrated knife to cut foam so it fits securely into liner, with the top of foam 1" (2.5 cm) below the basket top. See the Step 2 illustration to cut out a small triangle notch from the foam in back to create a space for daily watering.

3 Arranging Greens: Using a sharp kitchen knife, strip the needles and bark from the bottom 2" (5 cm) of each length. Push the evergreen pieces stems down into the floral foam, beginning in the center of the basket. Continue filling the basket, varying the kinds of greens and cutting the pieces shorter as you work out to the edges. Pieces on the edges are about 5" (12.5 cm) tall.

4 Light Clusters: Cut the 24-gauge wire into 12" (30.5 cm) lengths; begin at the end opposite the plug. Count over 2 lights, and refer to the Step 4 illustration to gather 6 light bulbs in your hand. Wrap wire 3 times around the cluster below the bulb bases, tightly enough to hold together, but not so tight that you damage the electrical cord. Twist the wire ends together to secure, tuck them in and trim. Leaving 2 lights between each cluster, and on each end, continue wrapping until entire string is complete.

5 Arranging Lights: Let the plug end dangle out of the basket; **do not plug in the lights.** Place the light string onto the basket of greens, and refer to the photo to push the clusters down into the greens so wires are completely hidden. Do not push them so far down that the lights or cord come in contact with the floral foam. Plug the lights in, and check the light arrangement.

6 Embellishing: Push the pinecones randomly, stem side down, into the arrangement. They should just rest in the tips of the evergreens; see the Step 6 illustration. Repeat to add the artificial berries.

7 Bow: Wrap ribbon around the handle, twisting gently. Cut, and hot-glue to secure. Make a large multiloop bow from remaining ribbon. Wrap the bow center with wire and wire to the basket at the bottom of 1 side of the handle.

8 Care: Water the basket every day, pouring slowly in the triangle-shaped hole in the back. Remember to unplug the string of lights first. Let the water soak in for at least 30 minutes before plugging in the lights again; never leave the arrangement unattended with the lights plugged in.

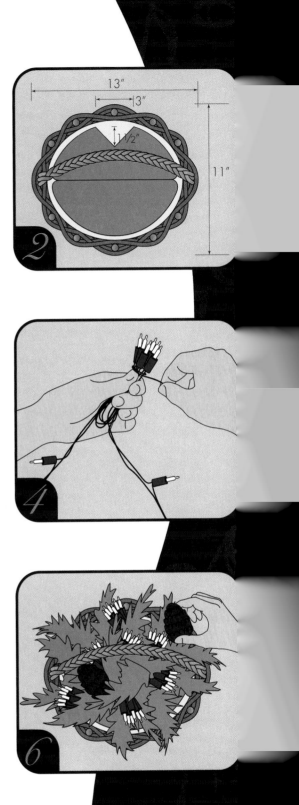

Cross-Stitched NATIVITY

The joy of the first Christmas has been beautifully crafted in this cross-stitched Mary and Baby Jesus. It reminds us of the true meaning of Christmas with its sheer simplicity. With a quilt-inspired background done in medium jewel tones, this design is only 5¹/₂" (14 cm) square, so it won't take a lot of time to do.

MATERIALS

- 14-count antique white Aida cloth, 11" (28 cm) square
- 1 skein each of 6-strand DMC embroidery floss in colors listed on Color Key
- Red metallic embroidery thread
- No. 24 tapestry needle
- Frame and mat, your choice
- Scissors

1 Refer to the Cross-Stitch General Instructions and Stitches on page 155 and the Stitch Chart to cross-stitch the design using 2 strands of floss.

2 Use a single strand of Vy. Dk. Beige Brown No. 838 to backstitch Mary and Jesus and a single strand of metallic red to backstitch the star and lettering. Mount and frame as desired.

NATIVITY STITCH CHART

Color Key

Symbol	DMC#	Color	Symbol	DMC#	Color
P	334	Med. Baby Blue	△	838	Vy. Dk. Beige Brown
S	351	Coral	N	913	Med. Nile Green
\	352	Lt. Coral	/	966	Med. Baby Green
○	369	Vy. Lt. Pistachio Green	X	3687	Mauve
=	434	Lt. Brown	J	3727	Lt. Antique Mauve
y	612	Med. Drab Brown	C	3743	Vy. Lt. Antique Violet
●	726	Lt. Topaz	–	3761	Vy. Lt. Sky Blue
V	746	Off White	—		Metallic Red Backstitches
⌐	754	Lt. Peach	—	838	Vy. Dk. Beige Brown Backstitches

Winter Welcome
MAILBOX

Painted in charming folk art style on a rural mailbox, here's a scene that says "welcome" in a very warm way. Mr. and Mrs. Snowman are waiting to greet you. There's a fire in the fireplace and a wreath on the door, so please come in, you're expected!

MATERIALS

- Rural mailbox, silver
- Acrylic paints: nightfall, dark forest, ivory, charcoal, tomato, forest green, maroon, yellow, cape cod
- Paintbrushes: Nos. 10 and 16 flat, Nos. 2 and 10/0 liner, No. 4 round scrubber, No. 2 round, flat scruffy
- Matte spray sealer
- Pattern Sheet
- Miscellaneous items: tracing and graphite paper, pencil, stylus, disposable palette, odorless turpentine, paper towels

1 Preparation: Lightly spray the mailbox and flag with 2 coats of sealer, following manufacturer's instructions. Let dry between coats. See Painting Instructions and Techniques on page 156 for all steps below. Trace the pattern onto tracing paper. Use the stylus and graphite paper to transfer the oval and house outline only to the mailbox side.

2 Oval and Hills: Mix a small amount of cape cod with nightfall and paint oval outline with liner brush. Let dry. Transfer hills, trees and house details. Use No. 16 brush to paint hills with a light ivory wash; see the Step 2 illustration. Use damp paper towel to quickly remove any paint beyond oval.

3 House and Sky: Use the appropriate-size flat brush or No. 2 liner. Paint the house side and front with ivory, the door and chimney with tomato, the windows with yellow and the roof with cape cod. Paint the door frame, shutters and attic window frame with cape cod. Paint the chimney side maroon. Paint the curtains and the chimney cap with ivory. Mix a small amount of cape cod with nightfall to lighten, and basecoat the remainder of the oval. Let dry.

4 House Details: Referring to the pattern, float on charcoal with No. 2 liner or round brushes to shade areas on house indicated by dots. Float ivory on random chimney bricks to highlight.

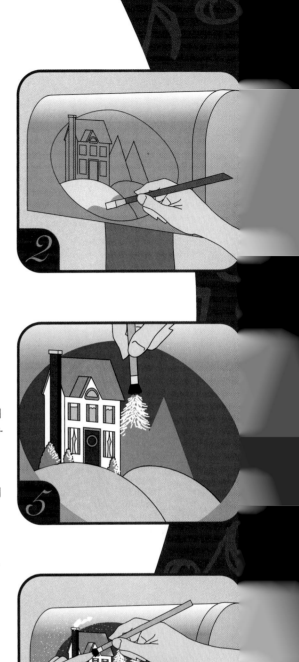

5 Greenery: Use the No. 4 round scrubber to dab forest green on the trees, bushes and wreath. Dab dark forest in centers and let dry. Pounce ivory on tree and bush edges using the scruffy brush; refer to the Step 5 illustration. Dab ivory highlights onto wreath.

6 Snow Couple and Lamp Post: Transfer remaining painting lines, and use No. 2 liner or round brushes. Paint the snow couple and snow-balls with ivory and the lamp light with yellow. Paint Mrs. Snowman's hat brim with tomato and crown with maroon. Lightly pounce tomato on cheeks. With charcoal, paint the lamp post and top, Mr. Snowman's hat and the buttons. Shade inside edges of snow couple, snowballs and lamp post with charcoal.

7 Shading: Use scruffy brush to dry-brush nightfall at the base of the door-way, lamp post, snow couple and between hills. Using the liner brush and charcoal, outline the oval outline, window panes, lamp light, attic window, shutters, door frame, roof and doorknob.

8 Snow, Smoke and Stars: Refer to the photograph and pounce ivory with scruffy brush onto roof for snow and above chimney for smoke. See the Step 8 illustration to use the scruffy brush to fleck ivory over entire side of mailbox, and liner brush to paint ivory stars.

9 Finishing: Paint "Welcome" with charcoal; use the liner brush and ivory to paint highlights. Let dry. Remove any remaining graphite lines by wiping lightly with odorless turpentine. Paint flag with 2 coats of maroon. Spray mailbox and flag with 2 coats of sealer, letting dry between coats.

Three Wonderful WREATHS

All who enter your door will be reminded by the jovial Reindeer to keep the Christmas spirit alive and ringing! Everlasting Plastic is an all-weather wreath made to withstand the elements outdoors and a great project for kids. Seashells gathered at the beach bring back summer memories.

MATERIALS

For Reindeer Bell Wreath
- 14" (35.5 cm) vine wreath
- Red raffia straw
- Three 2½" (6.5 cm) gold reindeer jingle bells
- 6-12 gold jingle bells, 10 to 15 mm wide
- 3 red berry clusters with leaves
- Glues: Thick white craft, hot glue gun

For Everlasting Plastic Wreath
- 1 box of 150 sandwich bags
- Lightweight wire clothes hanger, or purchased wire wreath form, 10" (25.5 cm) diameter
- 5" (12.5 cm) red velour bow
- 10" (25.5 cm) floral paddle wire

For Shell Wreath
- 12" (30.5 cm) grapevine wreath
- Assorted seashells
- Pearl finish spray
- 1½" (3.8 cm) reversible red gingham/velvet ribbon, 1 yd. (0.95 m)
- Hot glue gun
- Miscellaneous items: scissors, pliers, bleach, water container

REINDEER BELL WREATH

1 Bow: Tie a 1″ (2.5 cm) thick bunch of raffia into a 10″ (25.5 cm) loop bow with streamers. When gluing, first use hot glue, then white craft glue for reinforcement on all items. Insert and glue 1 berry cluster stem into 1 reindeer bell hanging hole and remaining 2 clusters into each side of bow knot.

2 Assembly: Refer to the photo to glue bow angled on wreath. Glue bell with berries above the bow, wherever it touches the wreath. Randomly tie remaining reindeer jingle bells to raffia streamers; see the Reindeer Bell Wreath illustration.

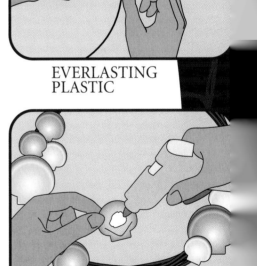

REINDEER BELL WREATH

EVERLASTING PLASTIC WREATH

Bend wire hanger to form a circle, using pliers, if necessary. Tie plastic bags onto wire, pushing bags together, until wire is completely covered; see the illustration. Pull and fluff sandwich bags. Wire bow to bottom right of wreath. Embellish as desired.

EVERLASTING PLASTIC

SHELL WREATH

1 Shells: Soak shells in bleach and water to clean; let dry. Spray shells with pearl finish following manufacturer's instructions; let dry.

2 Assembly: Refer to the photo and the Shell Wreath illustration to arrange and hot-glue shells around wreath. Tie a large 2-loop bow from ribbon and hot-glue to wreath. Hot-glue a shell in center of bow knot.

SHELL WREATH

NINE PINES
Wall Hanging

This fast-fuse pine tree wall hanging will remain a classic Christmas decoration throughout the years—just like the everlasting evergreen whose design is its inspiration. Created with different fabric ribbons that are woven and then fused in place, this quilt only looks pieced, and thus takes very little time to create. You won't even need a sewing machine, only an iron.

MATERIALS

- ¾ yd. (0.7 m) muslin, 45" (115 cm) wide
- Fabric ribbon, 1¼" (3.2 cm) wide: 2½ yd. (2.3 m) green print
- Fabric ribbon, ⅞" (2.2 cm) wide: 4¼ yd. (3.9 m) red plaid, 3 yd. (2.75 m) blue print, 4¼ yd. (3.9 m) floral print
- Rotary cutter and mat
- Transparent quilting ruler with 45° marks
- 22" x 26" (56 x 66 cm) craft fleece
- Heavy-duty fusible web tape: 5 yd. (4.6 m), ⅝" (1.5 cm) wide; 7½ yd. (6.9 m), ⅞" (2.2 cm) wide
- ¾" (2 cm) brass heart charm
- Miscellaneous items: tape measure, straight pins, iron, scissors, white craft glue

1 **Cutting and Preparation:** Cut two 22" x 26" (56 x 66 cm) pieces of muslin for wall hanging front and back. Cut four 26" (66 cm) lengths each from blue print and red plaid ribbon. Cut two 22" (56 cm) lengths from red plaid ribbon. Fuse 7/8" (2.2 cm) fusible web tape to the blue print and red plaid lengths and to the light floral ribbon, 1 yd. (0.95 m) at a time. Remove paper backing from floral ribbon and cut into fifty-six 2⅝" (6.8 cm) strips.

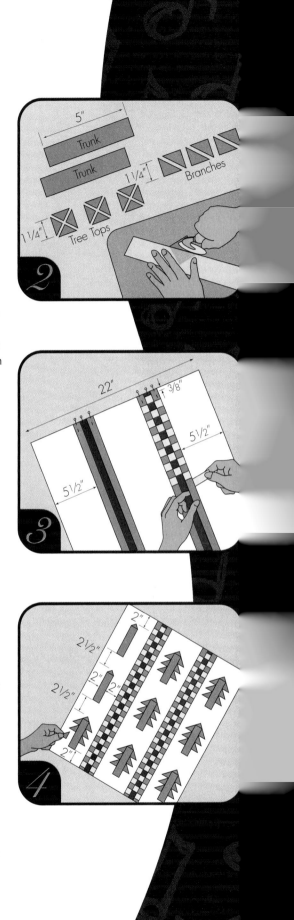

2 **Cutting Trees:** Cut two 2½ yd. (2.3 m) pieces of ⅝" (1.5 cm) fusible web tape. Follow manufacturer's instructions to fuse, overlapping slightly, to wrong side of green print ribbon. Remove paper backing. Rotary-cut nine 5" (12.5 cm) strips and thirty 1¼" (3.2 cm) squares. See the Step 2 illustration to cut 3 of the squares in fourths by cutting in half diagonally both ways to make tree tops. Cut the remaining 27 squares in half diagonally to form the triangle branches.

3 **Ribbon Weaving:** Measure and pin-mark 5½" (14 cm) in from the sides along the 22" (56 cm) muslin wall hanging front. Place a piece of blue ribbon inside the marks, and pin. Place and pin a red plaid ribbon inside the blue ribbons, then another blue ribbon. See the Step 3 illustration. Weave 28 light floral ribbon strips through the blue and red ribbon sets. Begin 3/8" (1 cm) from top and bottom edges and alternate the rows, referring to the photo. Fuse all ribbons when all edges are even and you are satisfied with placement.

4 **Fusing Trees:** Place the 5" (12.5 cm) green print tree trunks and triangle tree tops 2" (5 cm) from the woven ribbon bands and 2" (5 cm) from the top and bottom edges of the wall hanging front; see the Step 4 illustration. The middle trees should be about 2½" (6.5 cm) from the top and bottom trees. Fuse the tree trunks and tops. Place 3 right triangles on each side of trunks for branches; fuse.

5 **Assembly:** Pin-mark the centers of the wall hanging front, back and craft fleece. Match all pin marks and outer edges, and layer as follows: back, fleece and top, right side up. Pin the pieces together. Fold a 26" (66 cm) red plaid ribbon piece in half lengthwise, and encase 1 side edge. Pin, and fuse to the front and then the back. Repeat for the other side, and on the top and bottom edges with the 22" (56 cm) ribbons. Glue or tack the brass star charm above a tree; refer to the photo.

Techniques

CROCHET STITCHES

Beginning Slip Knot
Begin with a slip knot on hook about 6" (15 cm) from end of yarn. Insert hook through loop; pull to tighten.

Chain Stitch (ch)
Yarn over, draw yarn through loop on hook to form new loop

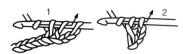

Double Crochet (dc)
1. For first row, yarn over, insert hook into 4th chain from hook. Yarn over; draw through 2 loops on hook.
2. Yarn over, and pull yarn through last 2 loops on hook.

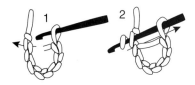

Forming Ring with a Slip Stitch
1. Insert hook in first chain.
2. Yarn over, and pull through all loops on hook.

Half Double Crochet (hdc)
1. For first row, yarn over, insert hook into 3rd chain from hook, and draw up a loop.
2. Yarn over, and pull through 3 loops on hook.

Single Crochet (sc)
1. For first row, insert hook into second chain from hook, and draw up a loop.
2. Yarn over, and draw through both loops on hook.

Slip Stitch (sl st)
Insert hook in stitch, and draw up a loop. Yarn over, and draw through both loops on hook.

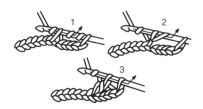

Triple Crochet (tc)
For first row, yarn over 2 times; insert hook into 5th chain from hook, and draw up loop.
1. Yarn over, and pull through first 2 loops on hook.
2. Yarn over, and pull through 2 loops on hook.
3. Yarn over, and pull through last 2 loops on hook.

Yarn Over (yo)
Wrap yarn over hook from back to front and proceed with specific stitch instructions.

CROSS-STITCH

General Instructions

1. Overcast the edges to prevent raveling. Fold the fabric in half vertically and horizontally to find the center, and mark it with a temporary stitch. If desired, place the fabric in an embroidery hoop. Find the center of the design by following arrows on the Chart. Count up and over to the top left stitch or specified point and begin stitching.

2. Each square on a Cross-Stitch Chart represents one square of evenweave fabric, unless otherwise indicated. Symbols correspond to the colors given in the Color Key.

3. Cut floss into 18" (46 cm) lengths. Separate the strands and use the number specified in the project. Stitching tends to twist the floss; allow the needle to hang free from your work to untwist it from time to time.

4. To begin, do not knot the floss, but hold a tail on the back of the work until anchored by the first few stitches. To carry the floss across the back to another area to be stitched, weave the floss under previously worked stitches to new area, but do not carry the floss more than three or four stitches. To end the floss, run it under several stitches on the back, and cut it. Do not use knots.

5. Work all cross-stitches first, then any additional stitches, including backstitches. Work in horizontal rows wherever possible. To make vertical stitches, complete each cross-stitch before moving to the next one.

6. When stitching is completed, wash the fabric in warm sudsy water if needed. Roll it in a terrycloth towel to remove excess moisture. Press it facedown on another terrycloth towel to dry.

STITCHES

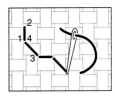

Backstitch
Up at 1, down at 2, up at 3, down at 4, stitching back to meet prior stitch.

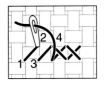

Cross-Stitch
Work first half of each stitch left to right; complete each stitch right to left.

Cross-Stitch
Stitch from lower left to upper right corner, then cross back.

Eyelet
Bring needle up in center hole of block. Then work around hole from outside back to center, pulling stitch to outside to create large center hole.

Smyrna Cross-Stitch
Up at odd, down at even numbers, working in numerical sequence.

EMBROIDERY STITCHES

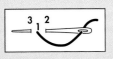

Backstitch
Up at 1, down at 2, up at 3, down at 1, stitching back to meet previous stitch.

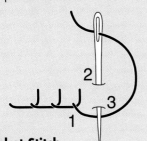

Blanket Stitch
Up at 1, down at 2, up at 3 with thread below needle; pull through.

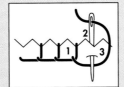

Blanket Stitch Inverted
Up at 1, around fabric edge at 2, up at 3 with thread below needle; pull through.

Blanket Stitch Corner 1
Make a diagonal blanket stitch. Tack stitch at corner, insert needle through loop; pull taut.

Blanket Stitch Corner 2
To work corner, use same center hole to work stitches 1, 2, and 3.

PAINTING

General Instructions

1. Sanding: Many projects are done on wood, and so must be sanded. If painting on a non-wood surface, make sure it is clean and dry. Begin the process with coarse-grit sandpaper, and end with finer grits. A 150-grit sandpaper will put finish smoothness on surfaces, such as preparing for staining or sanding. A 220-grit extra-fine sandpaper is good for smoothing stained or painted wood before varnishing, or between coats. Use a tack cloth—a treated, sticky cheesecloth—to lightly remove sanding dust after each step. Don't rub over the surface or you will leave a sticky residue on the wood. Wood files, sanding blocks and emery boards can be used to sand hard-to-reach places and curves.

2. Transferring: Place pattern on surface or wood, following direction for grainline. For pattern outlines, such as for cutting your own pieces, use a pencil to trace around pattern piece onto wood. Trace lightly, so wood is not indented. To transfer detail lines, you can use pencil, chalk, transfer paper or graphite paper. Ink beads over many waxed transfer papers, so if you plan to use fine-line permanent-ink markers for detail lines, be sure to use graphite or wax-free transfer paper. Transfer as few lines as possible, painting freehand instead. Do not press hard, or surface may be indented. Use eraser to remove pencil lines, damp cloth on chalk, and paint thinner or soap and water on graphite.

To use pencil or chalk, rub the wrong side of traced pattern. Shake off any loose lead; lay pattern penciled or chalk-side down on wood, and retrace pattern with a pencil or stylus.

To use transfer or graphite paper, place paper facedown on wood, then place pattern on top. Lightly trace over pattern lines. Lay a piece of wax paper on top of pattern to be traced. This protects your original traced pattern and also lets you see what you have traced.

3. Brushes: The size should always correspond in size to the area being painted, preferably with the largest brush that will fit the design area. The brush should also reflect the technique being done, which is usually suggested in craft project directions.

4. Extender: Acrylic extender is a medium to add to acrylic paints to increase their open time. Open time refers to the amount of time in which you can mix and blend the paints before they begin to dry. Those familiar with oil paints are most concerned with this, or if you are doing very complex designs with a great deal of shading.

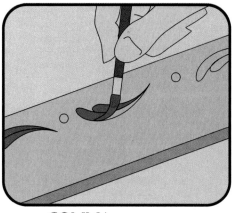

COMMA
STROKES

Techniques

Basecoating:
Applying the first coat of paint to a prepared surface, usually covering the surface and all edges in entirety. Sometimes two coats of paint are recommended. Basecoating is usually done with a flat or sponge brush.

Comma Strokes:
This is a stroke that is in the shape of a comma, with a large head and long, curvy thin tail. They come in all shapes and sizes. Begin painting up at the round head and curve down to the tail. Comma strokes require practice before they look right.

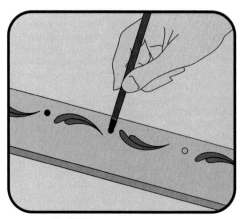

DOTS

Dots:
Dots can be made by dipping the end of the paintbrush or stylus or even a toothpick in paint and then touching it gently on the painted surface. This technique can create perfect eyes or dots better than any brush tip.

Double Loading:
This is the same as side loading, except two colors are loaded, one on each side of the brush. The colors gradually blend into one another in the middle of the brush.

Dry-Brushing:
This technique is used to achieve a soft or aged look; many times it is used to blush cheeks. Dip dry brush tips in a small amount of paint (undiluted for heavy coverage and diluted for transparent coverage). Wipe on paper towel until almost no paint is left. Then gently brush on the surface.

Highlighting:
Highlighting is the reverse of shading, causing an area to be more prominent. Thus a lighter color, such as white, is often loaded on a flat brush and used for highlighting. Highlighting is also sometimes done with a liner brush, by painting a straight line with a light color over an area to give a dimensional appearance.

Shading:
Shading is done with a color darker than the main color, making an area recede into the background. It is frequently used on edges of designs and done with the side load or floating technique. On an orange background, the brush is loaded with rust, and pulled along the edge, with the paint edge of brush where color is to be darkest.

Side Loading or Floating Color:
Side loading or floating is usually done with a flat or shader brush. Dip or load brush in water; then lightly blot on paper towel to release some moisture. Load or pull one side of the brush through paint. Blend paint on a mixing surface so the color begins to move across the bristles, and is dark on one edge, but light on the other. Make sure to get the paint well blended before actually painting on the surface. Another method is to thin the paint (see below) and mix it well. Load the paint by dipping one corner in and blending well on a mixing surface, as above.

Stippling (or Pouncing):
This is a stenciling technique, and is very similar to dry-brushing, except it gives a more fuzzy or textured look. Stencil, fabric or stippler brushes may be used, or any old scruffy brush. Dip just brush tips in a small amount of paint; then blot on paper towel until brush is almost dry. Apply the paint to the surface by pouncing up and down with the bristle tips until desired coverage is achieved.

Thinning:
Add drops of water and mix until the paint is of an inklike consistency. Sometimes a specific mix of water and paint is requested.

Wash:
Dilute the paint with five parts water to one part paint (or whatever proportion is requested) and mix well. Load the brush, and blot excess paint on brush onto a paper towel. Fill in the area to be painted, giving transparent coverage. A wash can also be used for shading or highlighting large areas.

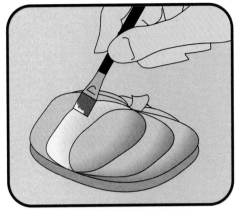

HIGHLIGHTING

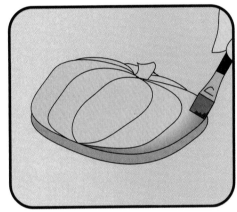

SHADING

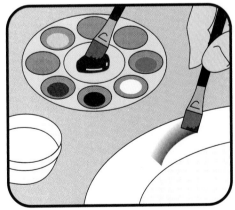

SIDE LOADING OR
FLOATING COLOR

PLASTIC CANVAS

General Instructions

1. Each line on a Plastic Canvas Chart represents one bar of plastic canvas.

2. To cut plastic canvas, count the lines on the stitch chart and cut the canvas accordingly, cutting up to, but not into the bordering bars. Follow the bold outlines where given. Use a craft knife to cut small areas.

3. To stitch, do not knot the yarn, but hold a tail in back and anchor with the first few stitches. To end yarn, weave tail under stitches on back; then cut it. Do not stitch over edge bars.

4. When finished stitching individual pieces, finish edges and join pieces as specified with an overcast stitch.

STITCHES

Beaded Half Cross-Stitch
Stitch from lower left, slip on bead, stitch down at upper right over 1 bar of canvas.

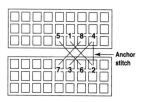

Braided Binding Stitch
Align edges; join peices with straight stitch, anchoring yarn in back. Up at 1, down at 2, up at 3, down at 4. Continue ending with straight stitch at opposite end.

Cross-Stitch
Sttich from lower left to upper right corner; then cross back.

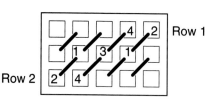

Continental Stitch
Work Row 1, up at 1, down at 2, up at 3, down at 4, working toward left. Work Row 2, up at 1, down at 2, working toward right in established sequence.

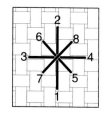

Double Straight Cross-Stitch
Up at odd, down at even numbers, working in numerical sequence.

French Knot
Up at 1, wrap thread once around needle, down at 1.

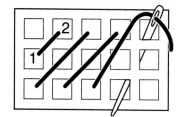

Gobelin Stitch
Up at 1, down at 2, working diagonal stitches over 2 or more bars in direction indicated on graph.

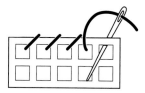

Overcast Stitch
Use a whipping motion over the outer bars to cover or join canvas edges.

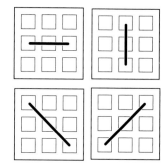

Straight/Diagonal Stitch
Stitch over specified number of bars as indicated on graph.

How to make a 14" (35.5 cm) pillow cover

1. Tapering Corners: Cut 15" (38 cm) square pillow back and front from white fabric. On the pillow front, make a chalk mark 3¾" (9.5 cm) from each corner along each side, for a total of 8 marks. At each corner mark a point ½" (1.3 cm) in from each raw edge. Make lines from the 3¾" (9.5 cm) marks to the corner ½" (1.3 cm) marks. Cut the pillow front along the lines, tapering to prevent baggy corners. Use pillow front as a pattern to taper corners on pillow back.

2. Assembly: Pin pillow front to pillow back, right sides together. Stitch ½" (1.3 cm) seam, leaving opening on 1 side for inserting pillow form. Turn pillow cover right side out, pulling out the corners. Press under seam allowances at opening. If desired, stitch in a 10" (25.5 cm) zipper following manufacturer's instructions, to make the pillow cover removable.

3. Finishing: Insert pillow form. Push fiberfill into the corners of the pillow as needed to fill it out. Zip pillow cover shut, or pin the opening closed and slipstitch shut.

Sources

Most of these items are available at your local craft retail stores. If you are having difficulty locating items, or live far from a retail store, please reference the sources listed below.

Page 6 Celestial Candleholder: Snowflake/Star Ornaments #16905, Octagon Candle Plate #17258 available from Walnut Hollow. Call 800-950-5101 or write 1409 State Road 23, Dodgeville, WI 53533-2112. Call or write Paragona Art Products, PO Box 3324, Santa Monica, CA 90408, 800-991-5899 for 16" x 20" (40.5 x 51 cm) sheets of Wire Form® Diamond Mesh. Designer Michelle Schmitz, courtesy of Walnut Hollow.

Page 8 Pin-Woven Christmas Cards: Provided by Wrights®; their bias tape, ribbons and trims were used. Cambridge Marking Systems ½" (1.3 cm) grid paper is available at 386 West 1600 South; Orem, UT 84058 or 800-747-5216.

Page 20 Paper Santa Trimmings: Provided by American Art Clay Co. Inc.; Cotton Press® cotton linter sheets, additive and terra-cotta Victorian Santa mold are all available from AMACO® at 800-374-1600.

Page 24 Christmas House Night-Light: Contact Plaid® at 800-842-4197 for: Gallery Glass™ 3-D House Blank #16210, liquid leading #16082 and Window Colors™: crystal clear #16001, snow white #16002, cameo ivory #16003, sunny yellow #16004, cocoa brown #16007, kelly green #16008, ruby red #16015, gold sparkle #16019 and ivy green #16024.

Page 34 Molded Wax Fish: Honey Wax® 100% Beeswax sheets in jade green NW-011, white NW-001, cinnamon NW-031, sunflower NW-028, Flex Molds® butterfly fish PM-615, sunfish PM-719, bass PM-720, mold release spray MD-396, 2/0 and 60-ply wicking and 3 g white pearlizer NW-200 available from Mann Lake Ltd, 501 S. 1st St., Hackensack, MN 56452-2001, 800-880-7694.

Page 64 Heavenly Ornaments-Angel: Provided by Wimpole Street Creations; their premade yo yos and Battenberg angels are available from Barrett House, PO Box 540585, N. Salt Lake, UT 84054-0585, 801-299-0700.

Page 68 Clay Angels: Friendly Clay™ and FIMO® polymer clays, and AMACO® Teddy Bear and Angel Doll Push Molds are all available from American Art Clay Co. Inc. Call 800-374-1600 for catalog.

Page 78 Handmade Paper Ornaments: Cotton Linter #29 sheets measuring 30" x 38" (76 x 96.5 cm) and weighing about 1 lb. (550 g) are only available by mail from Twinrocker Handmade Paper, PO Box 413, Brookston, IN 47923; 800-757-8946. Cotton Press® cotton linter sheets measuring 7" x 9½" (18 x 24.3 cm) and additive, are available at retail and by mail from American Art Clay Co. Inc. Call 800-374-1600 for catalog. 4 Cotton Press® sheets equal 1 Twinrocker sheet.

Page 92 Nordic Table Runner: Call National Nonwovens at 800-333-3469 ext. 214 for retailers who carry WoolFelt® by the yard. Norwegian blue 579, black 1000, hunter green 741, bright red 938, white 1100 and gold 416.

Page 100 Birdhouse Christmas Village: Stoves and Tinware Med. Cloud Cabin #11105, Livery Med. Birdie Barn #11111, Hotel Med. Flock Home #11102, Bank Med. Diamond Nest #11108, Antiques Med. Sunny Chalet #11114 and Barber Med. Wren Cottage

#11117. Call Walnut Hollow at 800-950-5101 or write 1409 State Road 23, Dodgeville, WI 53533-2112.

Page 106 Snowflake Vase: Mexican Pottery Clay™ is available from American Art Clay Co. Inc. Call 800-374-1600 for catalog.

Page 110 Cup of Tea Corner Shelf: Christmas Corner Shelf #63026 prestained green or #12878 unstained wood, Little Wood Tea Cups #30043 (sold in pairs) available from Walnut Hollow. Call 800-950-5101 or write 1409 State Road 23, Dodgeville, WI 53533-2112. Rubber stamps: Liberty Cup #808, Liberty Tea Pot #809, Casino Daisy #1109, Circle #603A available from Camp Stamp USA; 1751 Andrea Ave., Carlsbad, CA 92008, 760-754-1068. Designer Michelle Schmitz, courtesy of Walnut Hollow.

Page 116 Goldie Lawn Angel: Provided by Dow Chemical Co.; their Styrofoam® shapes were used. Cake dummies are available where specialty cake baking supplies are sold. 6" x 24" (15 x 61 cm) foam cones may need to be special-ordered at your local craft store or florist.

Page 128 Mantel Pendulum Clock: 6" (15 cm) square planter box #11225, Pendulum clock movement (hands included) #TQ800P, Graphite paper #1095 and 4½" (11.5 cm) Roman adhesive clock face (optional) are all available from Walnut Hollow. Call 800-950-5101 or write 1409 State Road 23, Dodgeville, WI 53533-2112. Designer Michelle Schmitz, courtesy of Walnut Hollow.

Page 132 Gold-Trimmed Velvet Stockings: Self-adhesive heart #14439; JOY self-adhesive wooden letters Times 14400 series: J #14409, O #14414, Y #14424; Fleur-de-lis Classic Dimensions #16110 (sold in pairs) available from Walnut Hollow. Call 800-950-5101 or write 1409 State Road 23, Dodgeville, WI 53533-2112. Designer Alison Stilwell, courtesy of Walnut Hollow.

Credits

Thanks to the following manufacturers for donating these craft projects for publication purposes.

Page 14 Ready-to-Wear Gingerbread: Provided by Duncan; their Scribbles® 3-Dimensional Fabric Writers and Brush 'n' Soft paint were used.

Page 84 Button & Bead Ornaments: Provided by Dow Chemical Co.; their Styrofoam® shapes were used.

Page 94 Clay Pot Christmas Tree: Provided by Duncan; their Aleene's Premium-Coat™ acrylic paints, varnish and Tacky Glue were used.

Page 104 Snowman Door Dolly: Provided by MPR Associates; their Creative Twist™ was used.

Page 112 Nutcrackers Sweet: Provided by Putnam Company; their pillow form, quilt batting and fiberfill were used.

Page 146 Cross-Stitched Nativity: Provided by DMC; their embroidery floss and metallic thread were used.